The
Jewish Way
of Life

The
Jewish Way
of Life

by
ABRAHAM J. KARP

Prentice-Hall, Inc., Englewood Cliffs, N.J.

PRINTED IN THE UNITED STATES OF AMERICA

50995—T

An Offering of Gratitude
to the blessed memory of
my father and teacher
AARON, son of ABRAHAM JOSEPH the Kohen
who entered life
the third day of Hanukkah, 5655
and was called to the Academy on High
the fifth day of Adar II, 5722

A Jew I Am . . .

In the letter to the king and queen of Spain with which Christopher Columbus begins the journal of his first voyage, he writes that in "the same month when Your Highnesses commanded me that with sufficient fleet I should go to the said part of India" the rulers of Spain "expelled all the Jews from your kingdoms and dominions."

Spanish Jews were confronted with the choice of conversion or expulsion.

Among the more than one hundred thousand who chose exile was a humble man whose name is unknown to history, but whose story was recorded by the chronicler Ibn Verga in *Shebet Yehudah:*

I heard from some of the elders who came out of Spain that one of the boats was infested with the plague, and the captain of the boat put the passengers ashore at some uninhabited place. And there most of them died of starvation, while some of them gathered up all their strength and set out on foot in search of some settlement. There was one Jew among them who struggled on foot together with his wife and two sons. The wife grew faint and died, not being accustomed to so much difficult walking. The husband picked up his children and carried them in his arms until he and they fainted from hunger. When he regained consciousness, he found that his sons had died also. In great grief he rose to his feet, raised his eyes to the heavens, and cried out:

"Lord of the universe, much have You done to make me desert my faith. But know this of a certainty, that a Jew I am and a Jew I shall remain! And nothing which You have brought upon me, or are likely to bring upon me, will be of any avail!"

Through the unnamed exile spoke the soul of eternal Israel. "A Jew I am, and a Jew I shall remain!"—even if the Almighty, as it were, was to be defied.

For thirty-five centuries this stubborn resolve has been the creed of a small people exalted by a grand vision and impelled by a divine destiny—the vision of the family of man redeemed; the destiny to become co-workers with the Father in the drama of redemption.

This vision drove the zealous band to brave the mountains of the spirit where no others dared to venture, there to covenant a partnership with a God who demanded total surrender —surrender which promised ultimate triumph. Their chosen destiny took them to new frontiers of human living, to new concepts of social enterprise and individual responsibility. It was an eternal vision, and the destiny could be fulfilled only in the "end of days."

Vision and destiny became divine duty. Duty to live on and serve on, "For if we perish, who shall be there to exalt Thy name?"

"I am a Hebrew," said the reluctant prophet Jonah, fleeing from God; and as though reminded by this statement of his duty to vision and destiny, he took up his prophetic office to preach God's word to a repentant Nineveh.

Centuries later the resolve was echoed by Rabbi Akiba as he cried out, "Hear, O Israel, the Lord our God, the Lord is One!" in the throes of martyrdom, his soul rising to its Source.

In our own time, Albert Einstein, an exile too, defying his people's tormentors, spoke these words of allegiance and affirmation:

> The pursuit of knowledge for its own sake, an almost fanatical love of justice, and the desire for personal independence —these are the features of the Jewish tradition which make me thank my stars that I belong to it.

Ancient prophet, medieval wanderer, and modern scientist —bound together in kinship of spirit which erases time and space, and makes of a hundred generations one undying people.

Determination and affirmation shaped the history of this people. Resistance and high resolve marked its way.

—The fleshpots of Egypt lured Israel back to the sweet irresponsibility of slavery;

—Baal and Astarte tempted the flesh with the promise of rich harvest and sensual delight;

—Ahur-Mazda's fires recruited them for the army of the blessed waging the good fight;

—The glory that was Greece enticed, and the grandeur that was Rome commanded:

—The Nazarene's cross offered life eternal, and the sword of the Prophet threatened;

—A new world offered new and alluring gods—

But to all, the words of the Faithful Wanderer:

"A Jew I am and a Jew I shall remain!"

This little volume will attempt in some measure to limn the vision and describe the destiny which have given life and purpose to this people. We shall learn how a people lifted up its eyes and its heart and saw what it was not given others to see; how it learned to know its God; how it came to understand what it means to love Him; how and why it took on the sanctifying discipline of a priest-people dedicated to the service of God. Above all we shall try to hear the call of the Faith to the Faithful. A call which all may hear, for it is eternal even as the people is eternal, and universal even as the One who calls them is universal.

We shall also come to know the anguish of the "eyes that see not," "ears that hear not," and "hearts that feel not." That the call often found no ready ears or open hearts, the prophet of old, the medieval moralist, and the rabbi of today bear sad witness.

And what of today?

There have been periods of our people's venture into history when the fire of faith burned more brightly, when the heart of the faithful beat more firmly, when the way of life of the Jew was purer, nobler, more exalted. But even in our generation as in generations past, we hear loud and clear:

"A Jew I am and a Jew I shall remain!"

And what in all of human history has been stronger and more fraught with promise than this resolve?

A great moralist of another century, in an introduction to a small volume that was to exert vast influence, wrote:

"I come not to teach you what you do not know. I come to remind you of that which you may have forgotten."

To Jews who have studied their faith, we shall attempt to recall what they may have forgotten. To those who had less to forget we offer information and elucidation. We pray that for both the Jewish way of life will provide knowledge and understanding, but above all, challenge.

Those who know Judaism only as the "mother faith," and whose interest and curiosity have not been matched by knowledge, will, it is hoped, come to comprehend Judaism as a way of life which has had as much vitality, meaning, and message during its second two millennia as during its first.

We shall call upon our tri-millennial literature, upon lawgiver, prophet, sage, scribe, saint, and scholar to illumine our way. Nor will we neglect the beliefs, practices, and legends of the common folk who constitute the people Israel.

The road this people has traveled in space and in spirit is long and varied. The soul of a people which lives, the substance of a faith which functions, are here to be presented to readers of all faiths.

Whatever success may greet this enterprise of exposition and elucidation is due to the vast treasures of heart and mind which are the heritage of this people. Where we shall fall short of our goal (as needs we must), attribute it to the breadth and vastness of the Jewish way of life, which humbles the wayfarer. Most humble of all is the chosen guide, who is aware of his inadequacy for the task, even as he responds to the duty to fulfill his calling as a "teacher in Israel."

He prays that the God who has been with his people in their journey in time and space and spiritual adventure will guide him in his efforts to recreate the landmarks of the Way.

"Life," said Oliver Wendell Holmes II, "is painting a picture, not doing a sum." Judaism, co-extensive with life, cannot be set down with mathematical precision through creed or catechism. Its mood and mode can at best be only suggested in a slim volume or even in a library of volumes. On the canvas which is the world in time and space, we have dabbed a few colors. The media and hues have been taken from a history which extends over three millennia and which has expanded over the inhabited region of the globe.

Quotations have been widely used. To quote "in the name of" is in the manner of the Jewish literary tradition. It conveys not only literal meaning but, what is equally important, it presents the idea or insight in its own unique nuance and with its own particular flavor.

We are grateful to the authors and publishers for permission to use quotations

From: *This Is My God* by Herman Wouk. Copyright © 1959 by the Abe Wouk Foundation. Reprinted by permission of Doubleday and Company, Inc.

From: *The Dybbuk,* by S. Ansky. By permission of Liveright, Publishers, N. Y. Copyright © R 1953 by Henry G. Alsberg and Winifred Kazin.

From: *Judaism And Christianity; The Differences* by Dr. Trude Weiss-Rosmarin. Published by the Jewish Book Club, New York, 1943.

From: S. M. Dubnow, *Jewish History*. Published by the Jewish Publication Society of America, Philadelphia, 1903.

From: *The Ethics Of Judaism* by Moritz Lazarus. Published by the Jewish Publication Society, Philadelphia, 1900.

It would be futility itself to attempt to list all the men and works whose words and views are distilled in this volume. We are deeply grateful to teachers and colleagues who have given us knowledge and insight into our faith and to the men and women of Congregation Beth El who challenge their rabbi to be an "eternal student" and encourage him to be a constant teacher.

Professor Selig Adler of the University of Buffalo, Professor Milton R. Konvitz of Cornell University and Mrs. Wilfred Wyler offered many helpful comments and suggestions; for their help and friendship, our gratitude. We are also grateful to all who read the manuscript—Dr. Robert Gordis, Dr. Simon Greenberg, Dr. Marshall Sklare, Rabbi Philip S. Bernstein, the Right Reverend George Cadigan and the Reverend Henry Atwell. The sympathetic interest of Mr. John Gudmundsen of Prentice-Hall, Inc. is also very much appreciated. Mrs. Mitchell Ostroff typed the manuscript with the efficiency of a secretary and the devotion of a friend.

Rabbi Abraham Burstein, a gifted writer and able editor, has given encouragement and help as only a loyal father-in-law can give. His daughter Deborah has inherited his literary talent, and this volume owes very much to her. In this as in so many things in life, she has been a devoted co-worker.

ABRAHAM J. KARP

Rochester, New York
June 1962.

Contents

1

THE ROAD

There is no God but God, and Israel is His prophet; not Moses, not Christ, not Mohammed but Israel, the race in whom God was revealed.

ISRAEL ZANGWILL

IN THE BEGINNING

Alone among the great religions of Western man, Judaism takes its name from a people. Christianity is named for its Savior, and Islam describes the way of the faithful. Judaism's name is derived from the tribe of Judah whose descendants constitute the Jewish people.

The very name of the faith suggests the centrality of the people with regard to it. Study confirms what the name suggests. It is important, then, to consider the people and the road it has trod.

A people's lifetime may be eternity, its habitation all the world. The people Israel has called itself an Eternal People; its faith has found new flowering on every frontier of an expanding world.

Man, of all the varieties of animal life, is the only one who knows not only what is, but also what ought to be. To know the Jewish Way of Life, we must know the life of the Jew as it was, and as his faith taught him it "ought to be." The life as it was affords background for understanding. The life as it ought to be is an ever-present challenge to the Jew to fulfil the pledge "We will obey and hearken," spoken at Sinai when a people met its God.

For more than thirty centuries this people has been dedicated to the enterprise of making actual the "ought to be." The task of making life match duty has met with varying degrees of success. But the attempt has ever been the chief pursuit, and the individual Jew has always judged his life by how near deed approached duty.

Hosea, the prophet of love, speaks of the relationship of God and His people Israel as a betrothal "in righteousness and justice, in lovingkindness and mercy." Which marriage has not had trials and troubles as well as joys and fulfilment; the coldness of estrangement as well as the warmth of comradeship? And often from the cold ashes of infidelity there burst forth the flame of faith, for the spark that united God and His people was never extinguished. Inscribed in the hearts of the people were the words of the Lord as spoken by the prophet:

"I betroth you to myself forever. . . ."

Let us now meet the Bride People of the Lord—the Jewish People.

EARLIEST MEMORIES

An eternal people lives with an abiding sense of history. From the history which a people records we can know them, for the historian is selective, recording that which he feels it is important to remember. What is it that this people chose to recall?

Joshua, mighty "man of spirit," having led the children of Israel into the Promised Land and having subdued it, divided the soil among the tribes and families. His work done, he gathered his people "before the Lord" and spoke to them in the name of the Lord:

> Your fathers dwelt of old time beyond the River, even Terah, the father of Abraham, and the father of Nahor; and they served other gods. And I took your father Abraham from beyond the River, and led him throughout all the land of Canaan, and multiplied his seed, and gave him Isaac. And I gave unto Esau Mount Seir, to possess it; and Jacob and his children went down into Egypt. And I sent Moses and Aaron, and I plagued Egypt, according to that which I did in the midst thereof; and afterward I brought you out.

In later times, when the Israelite farmer brought his first fruits to the Temple in Jerusalem as an offering to God, he would recite the following passage from the Book of Deuteronomy:

> A wandering Aramean was my father, and he went down into Egypt, and sojourned there, few in number; and he became

there a nation great, mighty, and populous. And the Egyptians dealt ill with us, and afflicted us, and laid upon us hard bondage. And we cried unto the Lord, the God of our fathers, and the Lord heard our voice, and saw our affliction and our toil, and our oppression. And the Lord brought us forth out of Egypt . . .

The earliest memories were then that the ancestors of the Jews came from "across the river" in Mesopotamia and that they sojourned in Egypt. In the former land they were idolators, in the latter, slaves.

The great civilizations of the ancient world were those which flourished in the "Land Between the Rivers" and on the banks of the Nile. They were brilliant civilizations, great in their accomplishments in science, mathematics, astronomy, architecture, and the arts. Calendar and pyramids attest their greatness. Abraham and his descendants lived in these empires and knew their civilizations.

The Bible records that God ordered Abraham out of his native land and its paganism, "to the land which I will show you," and that God plucked the children of Israel out of their slavery in Egypt.

Between these two great civilizations of the ancient world was a small land of hills and valleys framed by mountains to the north, the Great Sea to the west, and deserts east and south. It lay at the very center of the known world, in the middle of what historians call the Fertile Crescent. This land was the crossroads of the ancient world, the funnel through which flowed goods and people, and ideas as well, from river empire to river empire which flanked it.

Among those who came to this land was a family of shepherds from the East, the family of Abraham. A period of drought sent his descendants down to Egypt, whose great river made her impervious to the fickleness of weather. Welcomed at first, they were later pressed into forced labor, building the store-cities of Pithom and Ramses. During a period of military and political upheaval, the slave people, led by Moses, effected their escape from Egypt and set out for their ancestral home-land, the land between the empires, a land "flowing with milk and honey."

We have spoken of empires, a people and a leader. But the biblical account adds one more to the list of *dramatis personae*. Indeed, the hero of the narrative—God.

It was God who sought out Abraham in Ur of the Chaldees and bade him leave his homeland and its way of life rooted in idolatry. It was God who ordered Moses to go to Egypt. It was God who made slaves cast off their chains and eschew slavery, though they were reluctant to do so. In the biblical account, history and religious teaching became intertwined. To the historian's chronicle of facts, the religious teacher adds moral judgments. History thus became for Jews a vehicle of religious instruction, as religious teachings may be couched in terms of historic experience.

We can understand the life of this people only when we recognize this intermingling of fact and spiritual interpretation in historic accounts. The journey of Abraham and the exodus from Egypt are not merely incidents in history, but constitute also spiritual adventures. One man, Abraham, under the prod-ding of God, rises above paganism. A people, in response to God's urging, rebels against slavery. God desires that man be free from the error of idolatry, and God demands that man free himself from domination by fellow man. God's demand and this people's response—at times "yea," at times "nay"—is the history of the Jewish people.

The earliest memories of this people are accounts of journeys from Ur and the Nile to the Land of Promise. But journeys, too, from error to truth and from slavery to freedom. Exciting as were the adventures of foot and staff, vastly more thrilling and important were those of mind and heart.

MAN AT THE MOUNTAIN

Moved by memories and lured by promise, hordes of slaves followed Moses into the wilderness: they, anxious to sip the milk and taste the honey which flowed in the Land of Promise; he, determined to fashion them into a people with a purpose and a destiny.

The exodus from the land of bondage, and a victory at the Red Sea, fired the people with enthusiasm for their leader, and fealty to the God of whom he spoke. The moment was right for confrontation and covenant. A people was made ready to meet its God.

> Ye have seen for yourselves what I did to the Egyptians and how I bore you safe on eagles' wings and brought you hither to Myself.

The people were introduced to God through their own experience. As they began their journey, they knew God as Liberator and Protector. Later they were to experience His presence in other manifestations. At the very beginning, the Jew learned that religious faith is acquired, as a modern Jewish theologian expressed it, "not by being reasoned to about God, but by experiencing God's power in making life worthwhile." But God's concern and protection was conditional.

> If ye will listen to what I say and keep My solemn Covenant, ye shall be My own treasure among all nations, for all the world is Mine.

Yesterday's slaves were charged with a national purpose: to keep the Covenant. But more, a great destiny challenged:

> Ye shall be a kingdom of priests for Me, a holy nation.

The liberation from Egyptian slavery was not so much a compassionate act of a Father who took pity on their present plight, as it was a gift of opportunity by a God concerned about His people's future.

At Sinai, a small mountain in the great wilderness, the People of the Covenant heard the first demands for fulfilment of the "if." The world knows them as *The Ten Commandments*. The rabbis later commented that these were given for all mankind. "Why were they announced in the wilderness? So that no nation could say, they were meant for us only." And, they added, when God offered these words, they were spoken in the seventy languages of mankind, so that all might hear the challenge and the charge.

THE TEN COMMANDMENTS:

I am the Lord thy God, who brought thee out of the land of Egypt, out of the house of bondage.

Thou shalt have no other gods before Me . . .

Thou shalt not take the name of the Lord thy God in vain . . .

Remember the Sabbath day to keep it holy. Six days shalt thou labor, and do all thy work; but the seventh day is a Sabbath unto the Lord, thy God; in it thou shalt not do any manner of work, thou, nor thy son, nor thy daughter, nor thy man-servant, nor thy maid-servant . . .

Honor thy father and thy mother . . .

Thou shalt not murder.

Thou shalt not commit adultery.

Thou shalt not steal.

Thou shalt not bear false witness against thy neighbor.

Thou shalt not covet thy neighbor's house; thou shalt not covet thy neighbor's wife, nor his man-servant nor his maid-servant, nor his ox, nor his ass, nor anything that is thy neighbor's.

In the flush of religious enthusiasm the people solemnly responded:

"Whatsoever the Lord commands, we will do and will obey."

Forty days later, the same people built an idol of gold before which they offered sacrifices, ate the sacrificial meal, and rose up to revel.

The Calf of Gold inscribed itself upon the national memory of the people. They learned that eternal vigilance is the price of faith. It made this people wary of instant conversion which like Jonah's gourd "came up in a night and perished in a night." The people learned that religious commitment is the product of painstaking preparation of mind and heart. It took Moses forty years to make this people ready for the responsibility which freedom and opportunity demand.

A frightened band of slaves, who with longing remembered the fleshpots of Egypt and who yearned for the milk and honey of Canaan, was transformed into an orderly, resolute confederation of tribes, ready and able to enter the Land across the Jordan. Led by Joshua, disciple and successor of Moses, the people conquered, divided, subdued, and settled the land.

Freedom was theirs and opportunity too. But there were problems also. The confederation was a loose one, each tribe having to fend for itself. The enemies who surrounded them were many. Now it was Ammon-Moab who raided and despoiled, now it was the growing power of the Philistines which crushed and subjugated and threatened to destroy. Crises brought forth leaders, called *Shoftim* (Judges), who rallied one or more tribes to face the enemy. They were a motley group, ranking from leaders of stature like Deborah and Gideon to the brigand-leader Jephthah, and a man of legendary physical strength and matching moral weakness, Samson.

What united the tribes were common historic memories and a shared religious faith. The great prophet-judge, Samuel, calling on both, was able to unite the people, albeit into two groups, the northern dominated by the tribe of Ephraim, and the southern, by Judah.

It is recorded that when the judge Gideon proved successful in battle, the Israelites came to him and said:

"Rule over us, you and your son and your son's son."

But Gideon said:

"I will not rule over you, nor shall my son rule over you. The Lord alone shall rule over you."

It is further written that when Samuel was old, the elders of Israel came to him and spoke:

"You are old, and your sons do not follow in your footsteps; now make a king for us to rule us like all the nations."

Samuel warned them:

"This will be the manner of the king who shall reign over you. He will take your sons and appoint them to be his horsemen, and to be his captains, and to plow his land, and to reap his harvest, and to make his instruments of war. He will take your daughters to be cooks and bakers. He will take your fields and vineyards and your olive groves. He will take the tenth of your flocks. And you shall become his servants."

Samuel was echoing the anti-monarchical sentiments which find frequent expression in the Bible. For the People of the Covenant, God is King and no other. A kingdom of priests and a holy nation should be ruled by no monarch but God.

But the threat of the Philistines was stronger than theocratic or democratic sentiment. The people persisted and Saul was elected and anointed first king of Israel.

David, man of the sword and man of the lyre, succeeded the hapless Saul. A man of great charm, ability, and enterprise, he united the north and south, expanded the boundaries, and established the capital in the city of Jerusalem. He proposed to erect a sanctuary to the Lord in the new capital, to be a national shrine and a symbol of the unity of all the tribes who gave allegiance to the God of Israel.

The actual building of the Temple was left to Solomon, son and successor to David, who set about to consolidate the kingdom. He undertook an ambitious program of public works, in the course of which the warning of Samuel became a reality. He also entered into alliances with neighboring kingdoms, bringing foreign princesses to Jerusalem as wives, together with their idols. For all his vaunted wisdom, he planted in his kingdom the roots of revolution and destruction—exploitation of the people and the practice of paganism. A rebellion succeeded in tearing away the northern kingdom during the reign of Solomon's son and successor, Rehoboam.

King followed king. There were good kings like Josiah, but

they were few. There were bad kings like Menasseh, and they, alas, were many. But kings do not make a nation. What of the people?

The people which entered the Promised Land were tribes of shepherds. The way of life they knew was that of the nomad. Nomadic life is a precarious existence, but nomadic society has its great virtues also. It is signalized by wide personal freedom, and a man is valued for what he is, and for what he can contribute to the group. Each man, too, feels responsibility for the welfare of the entire group, and all know that in the well-being of the whole the individual will find security. There is a high sense of morality and family solidarity in nomadic societies. There is sharing and living together with each other and for each other.

The God of wanderers is not the god of a specific locality, but one who fills the earth, who is present wherever the tribe may pitch its tents and graze its flocks. Because the real worth of man is not in what he may be able to amass, but in how much he can contribute to the common good, the God of the nomad is not a god who gives but one who demands. A god who gives wants gifts. A god who demands seeks response. Such a God these wanderers met at Sinai. The Ten Demands were increased and multiplied through pronouncements, laws, and regulations. The ear of the nomad was attuned to such demands; his life had trained him for proper response.

The Land of Canaan, which these tribes possessed, supported an agricultural society. The physical life of the farmer was more stable and more secure. But for the life of the spirit it was fraught with danger. Group solidarity diminishes as each farmer attempts to extend his bounds. Property becomes all important, often at the expense of human rights. A man is judged more for what he has been able to amass, than for what he can contribute. There is always the real and present danger of the few owning much, and the many having little.

The farmer, dependent as he is on fickle nature, seeks ways and means to harness and to control it. He learns the art of plowing, fertilizing, sowing, irrigating, and reaping. But drought teaches him that this is not enough. He has to propitiate the gods of earth and sun and rain. They demand gifts. A Moloch asks for children, gods of fertility want orgies. Economic dislocation and immoral and sometimes inhuman worship marked the ancient agricultural societies.

When the nomads who entered Canaan became farmers, they learned how to harness nature. They were also taught by the native inhabitants how to "control" it through idolatry. And although laws, magnificent in concept, were pronounced to forestall economic injustice, the temptation was strong for the powerful to breach them.

But what of the Divine Experiment which began when God spoke to Abram in Ur and which was covenanted at Sinai?

A people remembers that which it wants to remember!

Who will remind this people of its purpose and its destiny?

Or as the prophet heard the voice of the Lord, saying:

> Whom shall I send,
> And who will go for us?

WHO SHALL SPEAK FOR ME?

Benjamin Jowett, Regius Professor of Greek at Oxford University, wrote:

> The moral feelings of men have been deepened and strengthened, and also softened, and almost created, by the Jewish prophets . . . The force of their words remains, and a light of heavenly truth and love streams from them even now more than twenty-five hundred years after they were first uttered.

It has been well said that no single group of men have had so profound an influence on the course of mankind as the prophets of Israel. The highest ideals of Western man are their legacy: justice, mercy, peace, one God and one humanity, the brotherhood of man.

They were the men who responded to God's call:

> Whom shall I send,
> And who will go for us?

Theirs was the conviction that God had ordained them.

> This day I give you authority over nations and
>   over kingdoms,
> To root up and to pull down, to destroy and to
>   overthrow,
> To build and to plant.

They were the spokesmen for God, re-echoing the demands God had made upon His people at Sinai. They examined the life of the people, judging it against the standard of God's will and words, indicating where they had failed in their response and what the consequence of failure must be. But more, they universalized God's call, and through this people spoke to all children of God, warning, pleading, demanding. The confrontation of prophet and people was a great drama for the instruction of the world.

Prophecy transcends history. Though the prophets spoke to a small people at a particular time in its historic development, because they spoke for God they proclaimed eternal truths, universal in application.

Who were these men, the prophets of Israel?

In ancient Palestine, the religious needs of the people were ministered to by priests who presided at sanctuaries. There were also itinerant dispensers of popular religion, who traveled in bands, interpreting dreams, predicting the future, and rousing the populace to religious enthusiasm. These were the early *nebi-im,* prophets.

In time some prophets would become attached to a king's court, serving in the monarch's regular retinue. So it was throughout the Near East. But among the Hebrews there were court prophets who were morally sensitive and utterly fearless. Such a prophet was Nathan in the court of King David.

David the King had done what many ancient kings were

wont to do. He appropriated another man's wife, after eliminating the husband. Nathan berated the king in the name of "The Lord, the God of Israel." The king listened, confessed, and repented his deed.

Which is the more remarkable and noteworthy: that Nathan the fearless prophet dared speak, or that David, the absolute monarch, listened?

David heeded the prophet's words because ingrained in the consciousness of the people was the conviction that God demanded justice, and that *no one,* even the great king, was immune to the divine order. In ancient Israel there was only *one absolute* monarch—God.

Among the itinerant prophets were solitary figures, singular in their vision, fearlessness, and passion for justice. Elijah, dweller in the wilderness, sought out King Ahab to condemn him for the murder of Naboth, whose vineyard he coveted.

"Have you found me, O my enemy?" said Ahab to Elijah. The prophet answered: "I have found you out. And the Lord has declared: 'Because you have given yourself to do what is evil in the sight of the Lord, I will bring evil on you.'"

When Ahab heard these words, he tore his clothes, put on sack cloth and ate no food. He fasted and repented of his crime. And he went about softly.

Martin Buber's insight is instructive.

"The prophet is appointed to oppose the king, and even more, history."

Let us then turn from kings to history.

In the middle of the 8th century B.C.E.* the Kingdom of the North, Israel, waxed rich and powerful. Jeroboam II had fashioned great victories, and payments of tribute flowed into the land. Commerce flourished and national feeling ran high. People flocked to the king's sanctuary at Beth-El for celebration and thanksgiving. A chronicler would have called Israel

---

* B.C.E. stands for "before the common era." It is equivalent to B.C. For A.D. the Jew uses C.E. or "common era," since A.D. (Anno Domini, the year of our Lord) would not be an appropriate statement for a Jew to make.

a happy kingdom, blessed with peace and power, wealth and well-being. Not so a prophet.

The prophet views the historical happening from the perspective of the divine demand. What did the prophet Amos see?

Prosperity is there in the land. For whom? For

> Men who crush the humble
> And oppress the poor . . .

Yes, there are peace and stability in the land, but

> The nobles and leaders of the nation
> Lie upon beds of ivory . . .
> And lap up wine by the bowlful
> With never a single thought
> For the bleeding wounds of the nation.

Courts of law abound, and judges too, who

> Browbeat honest men
> And accept bribes
> And cheat the poor of justice.

Religion is in high repute, the sanctuaries are crowded, where

> They lay themselves down beside the altar
> Upon clothes taken from the poor in pledge.
> And in the house of their God the priests drink
> The wine of them that have been fined.

"This is what *I* see," said the prophet to the people. And he also told them what God demands.

> Hate evil and love the good
> And establish justice in the gate
> Seek good and not evil, that ye may live.

But the words of the prophet go unheeded, and the prophet himself is ordered:

> Be off to the land of Judah,
> Play the prophet there!

For Judah, Amos has hope, but Israel—

> Israel is to be led off into exile,
> Far from their own country.

The prophets taught:

A nation's wealth is not synonymous with the people's welfare, nor does military might spell security. Every army will meet its conqueror, and every conqueror will despoil the land. But if a people remains firm in its faith, if its inner spirit remains strong, it can grasp victory out of defeat—the victory of survival.

History records military defeat; prophecy prepares a people for spiritual victory.

Amos warned of defeat and exile. His younger contemporary Hosea promised return and revival. He was no less sensitive to the sins of the people, and he was just as certain that deserved punishment would be meted out.

> The Lord has a quarrel with the inhabitants of the Land,
> Because there is no truth, nor mercy,
> Nor knowledge of God in the land.

But whereas Amos knew God as a Righteous Judge, Hosea saw God as a loving Husband of His bride people Israel. The prophet knew that Assyria's threat would soon become reality. But he also knew that God would not utterly reject his people. Will not a loving husband welcome back his bride who has been unfaithful? Reconciliation will follow chastisement.

> I will repeople Israel in the land,
> And I will have mercy on them that had not obtained
>   mercy;
> And I will say to them that were not my people:
> "Ye are my people."
> And my people shall say:
> "Thou art our God."

God is Justice, thundered Amos.
God is Love, consoled Hosea.
Amos and Hosea both are prophets of Israel.

Exile

The Kingdom of Israel fell to Assyria's might in 722 B.C.E. Samaria, the capital, was destroyed. The people, cast into exile, became the Ten Lost Tribes. Prophecy, alas, found fulfilment. Judah to the south beheld the fate of its larger and stronger sister nation and trembled. Its kings, in a desperate effort to save the nation, played the often fatal game of choosing the winner in the war of empires. Now it was allied with Egypt, now it paid heavy tribute to Assyria. But a powerful ally is never satisfied, and the enemy vows vengeance.

Isaiah, the prophet, lived and preached in Jerusalem in these perilous times. Angered Assyria was a threat, but the prophet saw yet a greater danger. Not political error nor military disaster, but moral decay, threatened the life of his people. A people can survive diplomatic misadventure, even defeat in battle. But a people snuffs out its own life when—

> God looked for justice,
> But there was only violence;
> For righteousness,
> But there was only the cry of the wronged!

Prophets have the power of sight and vision. Sight is to see things as they are. Vision is to see them as they might be and ought to be.

The world Isaiah saw was an armed camp. Egypt and Assyria were mustering strength and gathering allies for the great battle which would give the victor mastery of the world. The smaller nations were like jackals waiting for the portion of the prey the ravening lion disdains. Intrigue, murder, and violence flourished in every land; and in Judah, even in holy Jerusalem, there were corruption and deceit.

But Isaiah the prophet was also a man of vision. And he was moved to dream this dream:

It shall come to pass in the end of days
That the mountain of the Lord's house shall be
Established as the highest mountain,
And shall be exalted above the hills.
All the nations shall flow to it,
And many people shall go and say:
"Come, let us go up to the mountain of the Lord,
To the house of the God of Jacob,
That He may teach us of His ways,
And we will walk in His paths."
For out of Zion shall go forth the Law,
And the word of the Lord from Jerusalem.
He shall judge between the nations,
And shall decide for many peoples;
And they shall beat their swords into plowshares,
And their spears into pruning hooks;
Nation shall not lift up sword against nation,
Neither shall they learn war any more.

Assyria and Egypt, footnotes to world history and no more! But the dream of the "end of days" lives and will live so long as the human spirit longs for peace and yearns for God's Kingdom on earth.

What the others foresaw, the prophet Jeremiah experienced. This "man of sorrows" saw Jerusalem destroyed, the holy Temple razed, the people of Judah driven into exile. But the sorrow was deeper still. His people, the people he loved, had brought this calamity upon themselves. He pleaded with them but to no avail. Entangling alliances, corruption, greed, dishonesty, and leaders false to their responsibility still marred their life. Exile there would be, but return also. The demand of the hour was to prepare the people for life in exile.

For all others, exile meant extinction. Only the Jewish people departed, lived, and returned. Again cast out, they survived to return once more, because they had been prepared for exile by their prophets.

The prophets taught that exile did not mean rejection by

God but punishment. Punishment over, God would restore His people.

Amos promised:

> I will bring back
> The exiles of My people Israel.

Jeremiah prophesied:

> Again will I build you, and you shall be built,
> O virgin of Israel . . .

Jerusalem was destroyed in 586 B.C.E. and the Babylonian exile began.

How does a people live in exile?

Jeremiah despatched a letter to the exiles in Babylonia:

> Build houses and dwell in them, and plant gardens, and eat their fruits; marry wives and raise up families . . . And seek the peace of the city whither I have sent you to be citizens. Pray to the Lord for it, for in the peace thereof shall you have peace.

The spirit of the exiles was sustained by the prophet Ezekiel. He taught that children would not long suffer for the sins of their parents and that the exiles should make ready for return.

Return they did, forty-two thousand strong, when Cyrus, the Persian monarch who had conquered Babylon, decreed in 538:

> Whosoever there is among you who belongs to God's people, let him go up to Jerusalem.

They settled the city and rebuilt the Temple. With them they brought two remarkable acquisitions, the Synagogue and the charge of Isaiah of the Exile:

> Behold! My servant, whom I uphold;
> My chosen one, in whom I delight.
> I have put My spirit upon him,
> He shall make the right to go forth to the nations.
> He shall not fail nor be crushed,
> Till he establish the right on the earth.

The Synagogue gave the Jew universality, for it enabled him to be with his God wherever ten of the faith met in prayer.

The words of the Second Isaiah gave this people immortality, for God now charged them with an eternal purpose, to be "a light unto the nations . . . till he establish the right on the earth." The prophet of the Exile taught the people that theirs was the responsibility to lead the world to fulfilment of the vision of "end of days" which his namesake had preached in Jerusalem.

In Israel's history, prophet replaced priest as servant of the Lord. The God of history now demanded that the kingdom of priests become a prophet people, proclaiming God's word to all the peoples. Israel was to be the servant of the Lord. A suffering servant to be sure, for such is the vocation of the prophet. Peace is not his lot, but glory.

RETURN

In Babylon's Exile the people cried:

> Our bones are dried up, our hope is lost!

Ezekiel consoled them and promised:

> Thus saith the Lord God: I will open your graves,
> And raise you from them, O My people; and
> I will bring you unto the Land of Israel . . .
> And I will put My spirit in ye and ye shall live.

By the rivers of Babylon a people sat and wept, "when we remembered Zion."

On return to Zion, "Our mouth was filled with laughter, and our tongue with singing."

Pioneer zeal added enterprise to enthusiasm. Houses were built, and foundations laid for the second Temple of the Lord. But enemies soon encompassed them and, alas, danger dampened enthusiasm and blunted enterprise.

The prophet Haggai challenged with words of the Lord:

> Take courage all ye people of the land!
> Courage! Do your work, for I am with you!
> A little while longer, and I will fill this
>   house with glory.
> And greater will be the glory of this house
>   than of the former.

"And they completed the building as the God of Israel commanded." Zechariah added a timely prophetic warning:

> Not by might nor by power, but by My spirit,
> Saith the Lord of hosts.

The reconsecrated Temple did not assure religious commitment or observance. A century later, when Nehemiah, disturbed by reports from Judea, arranged to go there as governor, he found widespread religious indifference and moral breakdown. The Sabbath was profaned, intermarriage was rife, and economic exploitation had turned brother against brother. Nehemiah, a man of devoutness and devotion to the welfare of his people, soon put an end to these abuses. He laid the foundation for the great religious reforms of Ezra, which gave new vitality to Judaism and thus assured continued life for the People Israel.

Nehemiah reports that in rebuilding the walls of Jerusalem, each workman, building with one hand, was always "ready with the other to grasp his spear." In the spiritual rebuilding, which was the task of Ezra, the program was the same. On the one hand, he had to preserve that which had been received, but on the other, he had also to fashion new forms and create new institutions which would give meaning, relevance, and life to the old.

Ezra was a *Sofer,* a man of the Book. Religious authority and leadership now moved from prophet to *Sofer.* The prophet exhorts, warns, challenges; the Sofer *teaches.* An impressive body of religious literature already existed: the laws and historical portions of the Pentateuch, scrolls which contained the words of the Prophets, the great evocations of the human soul which we now call the Psalms. The *Soferim* gathered the manuscripts, edited them, and, what is most important, taught their contents to the people.

The Book of Nehemiah records one of the most significant revolutions in the history of man's spiritual adventure.

> Ezra brought the book of the Law of Moses before the congregation, both men and women, and all that could hear with understanding . . . And Ezra read in the Book from morning until midday; and the people listened carefully to the book of the Law. And the Levites instructed the people in the Law . . . and explained its meaning and caused the people to understand the reading.

Religion was no longer the sacred prerogative of priests, nor even the inspired preachments of the prophets. It was the responsibility of all the people, "men and women, and all that could hear with understanding." Its teachings were not the preserve of priest or prophet but the "inheritance of the Congregation of Jacob." Instruction came from Scripture which was available to all, and whose study now became a religious duty. "The object steadily aimed at was the elevation of the whole body of the people to the plane of spirituality, its transformation, in accordance with the Biblical injunction, into a 'kingdom of priests.' "

The historian Simon Dubnow calls this period "the school days of the Jewish nation." The *Soferim* taught, the people studied. The text was the Book. "Their progress was brilliant," he writes, "and when their schooling had come to an end, and they stepped out into the broader life, they were at once able to apply their knowledge successfully to practical exigencies. They were prepared for all the vicissitudes of life. The spiritual equipment was complete."

The people learned Judaism, and Judaism reaffirmed its conviction that a religious way of life can not be *caught,* it must be *taught.* It is not the product of a moment's decision, but the result of a life-long pursuit. For Judaism, the religious way of life of the Jew, embraces all of life. It encompasses the adherent's existence "from the rising of the sun to the going down thereof," and from the cradle rocked by the mother to the one provided by mother earth.

Ezra and Nehemiah found a people estranged from faith. The *Soferim* produced a body of believers who directed their lives by the demands of the Law. An undisciplined band of pioneers had been fashioned into a religious community strong in faith and exalted in behavior. Small wonder then that Ezra the Sofer is called "the second Moses."

RESISTANCE AND REBELLION

Legend has it that Alexander the Great, little more than thirty years of age, died of a broken heart because he had no worlds left to conquer. This student of Aristotle, enamored of the Greek Way, sought to hellenize (or "grecianize") the lands he subjugated. Convinced that Hellenic civilization would stabilize the empire, he harnessed the might of the empire to bring it about. The division of the world among his generals after his death placed little Judea between two aggressive monarchies in Egypt and Syria.

The Syrian king, Antiochus IV, who proudly titled himself Epiphanes (Enlightened One), sought to impose the light of Greek culture upon the inhabitants of Judea. Many among the aristocracy and the wealthy became more Greek than the Greeks. But the *Soferim* had taught well. The people resisted the lure of Greek glow and glitter, and when the tyrant sought forcibly to impose it upon them, they rose in rebellion.

Why the resistance and rebellion?

We call again on the historian Dubnow.

Hellenism was the first gravely dangerous opponent Judaism had to encounter. It was not the ordinary meeting of two peoples, or of two kinds of civilization. It was a clash between two theocracies of life that stood abruptly opposed to each other, and were, indeed, mutually exclusive. It was a duel between "the Eternal" on the one side, and Zeus on the other—between the Creator of the universe, the invisible spiritual Being who

had, in a miraculous way, revealed religious and ethical ideals
to mankind, and the deity who resided upon Olympus, who
personified the highest force of nature, consumed vast quanti-
ties of nectar and ambrosia, and led a pretty wild life upon
Olympus and elsewhere. In the sphere of religion and morality,
Hellene and Judean could not come close to each other. The
former deified nature herself, the material universe; the latter
deified the Creator of nature, the spirit informing the material universe. The Hellene paid homage first and foremost to
external beauty and physical strength; the Judean to inner
beauty and spiritual heroism.*

The Hellenic theory identified the moral with the beautiful
and the agreeable, and made life consist of an uninterrupted
series of physical and mental pleasures. The Judean is per-
meated by the strictly ethical notions of duty, of purity, of
"holiness"; it denounces licentiousness, and sets up as its ideal
the controlling of the passions and the infinite improvement of
the soul; not the intellect alone, but the feelings as well.

When religious persecution was added to political oppression, the "Pious," led by a family of priests, rose in rebellion,
in 168 B.C.E. The rebellion succeeded in ridding the land
of the enemy, in purging the nation of Hellenism, and in
setting up an independent state under the priest-kings, the
Maccabees. Power corrupted, and dynastic quarrels supplanted
religious ardor and sacrifice. The state disintegrated, but not
before the power of Rome was invoked during a political con-
troversy. Invited to help, Rome remained to subjugate and
dominate.

The Maccabee rulers were both the political and ecclesiastical heads of the nation. The aristocracy of position and
possessions was interested in the political aspects of national
being. A strong state, with ever-widening borders, served its
interests best. The well-placed exerted their influence to assure
that the Maccabee prince be first and foremost an ambitious
monarch. Religious practices were adhered to, strict and un-

* S. M. Dubnow, Jewish History, the Jewish Publication Society of
America, Philadelphia, 1903.

changing, largely because they gave stability to the state. The populace, on the other hand, looked to the descendants of the Maccabees for religious leadership. The state was desirable insofar as it gave the people full opportunity to practice their religion freely and to develop and expand it until it infused all of society and informed every act of the believer. Out of these two groups with their diverse interests grew the two great parties of the time, the Sadducees, aristocratic, dogmatic, unchanging; and the Pharisees, concerned with the life of the people, pragmatic and practical in religious views and usage, and devoted to the proposition that Israel was a priest people bound in service to God to establish His kingdom on earth.

Pharisaism saved Judaism. Indeed, it became Judaism. Its leaders knew that national survival lay not in political power but in religious commitment and discipline. So the prophets had taught. So life demonstrated. But national survival was for a purpose, "for if we perish, who will glorify Thy name?" What better way to glorify God's name than to make His presence manifest in every act of the believer, and in the laws which regulated the life of the community of the faithful? So laws multiplied and the legal system touched on every aspect of life. Pharisaic law flowed out of an inner spirit wholly dedicated to the service of God. The Pharisees were architects of the Jewish way of life, and much which we shall discuss in the later chapters of this volume is their legacy.

Rome was mistress of the world. The *pax romana* which little Palestine knew was the peace of the sword. Rome demanded submission and had the power to enforce it. The mass of the people yielded grudgingly, waiting for better days. There were also the Zealots who preached rebellion, and small sects who awaited the imminent coming of the Messiah and establishment of God's Kingdom on earth. Zealots and acclaimed messiahs were immolated on Roman crosses as a warning to the populace not to disturb the peace.

Among the men who preached the doctrine that the "end

of days" was at hand, and that men must prepare to meet
their Maker, was a young Galilean, Jesus of Nazareth. He was
a devout Jew, faithful to the Law and the doctrines of Judaism,
preaching to his disciples: "For verily I say unto you, till
heaven and earth pass away, one jot or one tittle shall in no
wise pass away from the law, till all things be accomplished."

He was convinced that "the time is fulfilled and the Kingdom of God is at hand." Men should turn their attention away
from this world, its weal and woe, its pleasures and its pains,
and prepare for "the Kingdom." In inveighing against religious
hypocrisy and social injustice, he echoed the words of the
Prophets. To love all men, even one's enemy, to answer evil
with good, and to see this world as but the vestibule of the
next are teachings found in Jewish tradition. But his unconcern
for this world, and his disinterest in its toils and tribulations
carried him off the road of Jewish tradition. The "end-of-the-
world morality" of Jesus was a deviation from the ethic-
centered way of life which Judaism is. Diverse emphases are
found in Jewish tradition, tolerated as detours which eventually
lead back to the main highway.

Jesus was a folk teacher and religious leader of rare ability,
and he attracted to himself and to his message a number of
Jews who became devoted disciples. Some began to think of
him as the Messiah, come to redeem man and to usher in the
Kingdom. His preaching grew bolder. Soon he came to the
notice of the authorities charged with preserving the peace,
and the Galilean was hanged upon the cross as others had
been before him. The man on the cross, under the mocking
sign, "King of the Jews," was condemned by Rome for
threatening its peace, and mourned by his faithful as the
Messiah.

The Nazarene lived on beyond the grave, at first a martyr
revered by a small Jewish sect. Later, his ministry and passion
became the center of a new religion preached by Paul to the
gentiles. Soon the gentile Christians outnumbered the Jews
and the daughter religion strayed ever farther from the mother,

discarding old disciplines and doctrines and taking on new. After destruction of the Temple, the breach was complete. The new religion went forth to convert the world.

Rome was a cruel mistress. Contemporary Jewish sources state:

> Roman civilization was all selfish: they built market places to harbor harlotry, baths for their own refreshment, bridges to exact tolls.
> When a swine lies down, it spreads out its paws, as if to say "I am clean!" So wicked Rome robs and oppresses, yet pretends to be executing justice.

The people were warned to steer clear of involvement with this cruel, immoral, rapacious empire.

A people who knew only God as king, could not render unto Caesar that which was Caesar's. A conflict between Rome and Jerusalem was inevitable, and it broke out in all fury in the year 68 C.E. Heroism could not overcome well-armed legions; Jerusalem fell and the Temple went up in flames in the year 70.

There is a folk tradition that on the day the Temple was destroyed, the Messiah was born. Rabban Johanan ben Zakkai shared this faith and gave it practical application. While Jerusalem was still besieged, he stole out of the city and established a school in the vineyard of Jabneh. Jerusalem fell to the enemy, but Judaism was saved by the school at Jabneh and its successor academies. The Jew lived on to remember conqueror and conquest as but another page in his millennial history.

The spirit of the Jew survived and transcended defeat. Hardly had the flames which consumed the Temple turned to ashes, than talk of freedom was again heard in the land. The Romans now attempted, as had the Greeks before them, to erase this people by eradicating its faith. The teaching of Torah and the practice of Judaism were forbidden under pain of death, and martyrdom on a new scale entered Jewish history. Continued oppression and persecution fanned the flames of rebellion. Rabbi Akiba himself gave it spiritual leadership, and Bar Kochba defied the Roman legions. But this people which had fashioned mighty spiritual victories could not prevail against armed might. The rebellion was cruelly crushed in 135. The people took up the wanderer's staff, and the long Exile began.

With them the wanderers took the synagogue, which became their portable homeland; the Law which disciplined their lives and united them in bonds of common living; and above all, a divinely ordained destiny which gave purpose to life and meaning to suffering.

JOURNEY FROM JERUSALEM

When the Holy One, blessed be He, remembers His children who are cast in sorrow among the nations of the world, He sheds two tears which fall into the Great Sea, and their sound is heard from one end of the world to the other.
Says the Holy One blessed be He: Woe to the children, for whose sins I destroyed My house, burned My Temple, and exiled My people among the nations . . . Woe to the father who banished his children, woe to the children who were banished from the table of their Father.

Thus the rabbis viewed destruction and banishment: a national calamity to be sure, but a cosmic tragedy as well.

Why was the First Temple destroyed? Becuase of idolatry, immorality and bloodshed. But in the days of the Second Temple, people studied the Torah and worshiped, and engaged in deeds of loving kindness, why was it destroyed? Because there existed causeless enmity amongst the people.

The Righteous Judge is bound to justice. Justice demanded defeat and exile. But the merciful Father would redeem and return.

R. Joshua of Siknin taught in the name of R. Levi:

The Holy One, blessed be He, took the words of the fathers, and fashioned them into the key which will open the gates of redemption to the children.

The rabbis knew that only the words of the fathers would sustain the children through the dark night of exile. The Bible was canonized, and the Oral Law, which had grown with the people and had been transmitted from master to pupil, was now reduced to writing. Rabbi Judah the Prince, who directed the enterprise, which was concluded about the year 200, saw the waning of the religious center in Palestine, and the growth of Jewish communities east and west. For these rising new centers he edited the Mishnah, a compilation of laws and opinions, which became the guide for Jewish religious, social, and civic life. The Mishnah was discussed in the academies and law courts in Palestine and later in Babylonia. The digest of these discussions is called the Gemara. Mishnah and Gemara together are called the Talmud.

The giants of the spirit who created the Talmud were faced with the formidable and unprecedented task of fashioning a stateless nation. The prophets spoke as they did, because God had made it historically imperative to denounce and pro-nounce—to denounce those aberrations which decreed na-tional doom, and to pronounce principles of justice, love, and destiny which assured life. The rabbis knew that their historic imperative was to translate the principles promulgated by the prophets into laws that directed life. The God of history demanded of the prophet that he preach, of the scribe that he teach, and of the rabbi that he legislate.

The Law grew till it touched every aspect of life. It taught the Jew how he might express reverence for God and loyalty to the Covenant through those activities of life we call common-place. The Law lifted the ordinary to the realm of the extraordinary. It made daily living a divine drama of man's response to the cosmic call. The Jew could serve God every day in every way.

NATION WITHOUT STATE

What are the requisites of nationhood?

Answer: A common history, destiny, law, language, litera-ture, government, and geographic proximity.

The Jew was conscious of the antiquity of his history. (Josephus had reminded him and the world of it.) What is more, he devoutly believed that God Himself was the central hero of his people's story.

As for his destiny, had not God proclaimed through His prophet of the Exile:

> I the Lord have called thee in righteousness,
> And have taken hold of thy hand,
> And kept thee, and set thee for a covenant of
>   the people,
> For a light of the nations;
> To open the blind eyes,
> To bring out the prisoner from the dungeon
> And them that sit in darkness out of the
>   prison house . . .
> That My salvation may be unto the end of the
>   earth . . .
> Ye are my witnesses, saith the Lord.

The Law was a legal system *par excellence,* informing the adherent how qualities of mind and heart could find expression in the arena of social living. Its spirit inspired lofty ideals, and more important, its letter instructed how these ideals might be translated into deeds.

Of languages there were two: Hebrew, holy in its antiquity and association; and Aramaic, the *lingua franca* of the ancient Near East, which the people spoke and which related the Jew to his neighbor.

Which folk could boast of a richer literature? Prophet, poet, sage, wisdom teacher, historian, legislator, and God Himself were its fashioners.

The government was composed of those to whom the people looked for leadership. In Palestine, the Patriarch; in Babylonia, the Exilarch, and everywhere the men who were masters of the Law.

For geographic proximity, which exile denied, the rabbis substituted the spiritual proximity effected by common daily rites and religious observance. A Jew never felt himself a stranger anywhere a fellow Jew lived. A resident of Baghdad would immediately feel at home in Cordova or Mainz, for he would find brethren with the same disciplines of diet, offering the same prayers in the same language, observing the same daily ritual, celebrating Sabbath and holidays in like manner, and discussing the wanderings of Abraham, the adventures of David, and the martyrdom of Akiba with the same sense of kinship as did fellow Jews in his native city.

The one aspect of nationhood which the Jew no longer had was Land and State. Law and Synagogue were now the wanderer's state. And in truth, he never left the land. When the Jew did not live in Palestine, Palestine lived in the Jew. He knew its hills and valleys, celebrated festivals tied to land and climate, directed his prayers toward Jerusalem and prayed thrice daily:

> Gather us from the four corners of the earth . . .
> And let our eyes behold Thy return in mercy to Zion.

Thus armed, this people journeyed from Jerusalem to the lands of the dispersion.

DIASPORA

It is estimated that at the time of the destruction of the Second Temple there were some four and one-half million Jews in the world. Great Jewish communities were already flourishing outside of Palestine. The Jewry of Alexandria was large in number, influential, cultured, and sophisticated. In North Africa, Spain, Italy, and even Russia there existed colonies of Jews.

The oldest and largest Jewish community in the Diaspora was in Babylonia. It enjoyed a wide degree of autonomy, while the Exilarch received official recognition from the government. That in matters of the spirit, Babylonian Jewry was preeminent as well is reflected in the Talmudic statement:

When the Torah was forgotten in Israel, sages came from Babylon and restored it—Ezra, Hillel, and Hiya and his sons.

Relationship with the mother community was close and cordial. Spiritual bridges existed between the two which gave strength and vitality to both.

The flowering of Babylonian Jewish scholarship came to bloom in the persons of Rav and Samuel. The former, Palestinian trained, was the expert in religious law: the latter, versed in medicine and astronomy, excelled in civil law. His dictum, "the law of the land is law" did much to make possible the integration of the Jewish communities into the life of the lands of their dispersion. This means that in matters of civil law (not religious) the Jew is duty bound to obey the laws of the state in which he lives.

The synagogue, a house of prayer, study, and assembly, was the central institution of each community. But what gave particular quality and character to Babylonian Jewry was its great institutions of higher learning in Sura, Nehardea and Pompedita. Most noteworthy about these academies is that they were made into institutions for popular education. During the two months of *Kallah* in spring and autumn, scholars, artisans, farmers, and merchants streamed to the academies to partake of the learning which flourished there. This was a remarkable occurrence, unmatched in the history of education. Many thousands left their work or business to spend two months each year in concentrated study. The learning and discussion not only informed the people, but also inspired its ablest sons to devote their lives to scholarship, for the scholar was the most revered and most significant member of the community.

It was not long before the heads of the academies became the really influential leaders of the community. This was particularly true during the second half of the first millennium. So important did these spiritual and intellectual leaders become, that they were accorded the title *Gaon,* Excellency. The religious authority of the Babylonian scholars was recognized by the other Jewish communities. They looked to the academies for religious guidance. In turn they accepted the responsibility to aid in their support. To Babylonia's academies came questions of law and usage. From them went forth scholarly fund collectors who became living links to unite the various communities. Contact and communication were constant.

By the turn of the millennium, however, the power and influence of Babylonian Jewry began to diminish. Political upheavals caused dislocation of communities and disruption of life. The center of the world was moving westward across the Mediterranean, and Jewish life with it.

Before leaving Babylonia, we must take note of two great challenges which faced Judaism, and the man who resolutely met them. From Arabia's desert came the first, the second from within the Jewish community itself.

The pent-up energies of the tribes which peopled the Arabian peninsula were loosed in the seventh century by the founder-prophet of Judaism's second daughter religion. Mohammed promised the Arab dominion in this world and blissful life in the hereafter. The sword of the faithful led the crescent in conquest. We hear of powerful Jewish kingdoms in Arabia, and these the prophet wooed. To do so, he incorporated into the faith Jewish rites and symbols, and proclaimed to "The People of the Book" (as he called them) that the God he called Allah was the God of Abraham, the God of The Book. The sword was bared in service of Allah, and with effect. But the greater danger arose from the crescent of faith. The Moslem world burst alive with intellectual activity so brilliant and exciting that it had considerable appeal for many Jews.

At the same time a "back to the Bible" movement made significant headway in Judaism. Karaism, as it was called, rejected the authority of post-Biblical tradition as found in the Talmud, and urged a return to the laws of the Bible, unchanged and unrefined. We can well imagine the appeal such a movement would have on "The People of the Book." There were those who became its adherents because it permitted them to throw off the yoke of Talmudic law. But they soon found that Biblical law in application was no less demanding, and often more restrictive. Talmudic law had developed with the people in response to their needs. It was continually undergoing the greatest test of all—acceptance. Centuries of history could not be erased, and Karaism, after the first flush of success, became a dwindling sect, with but a handful of adherents surviving to the present. The instinct of the rabbis for national life and survival was vindicated.

The challenge of a vital force cannot be ignored. Those who emulate the legendary ostrich soon find that the covering sands, which at first seem to offer sanctuary and protection, stifle and eventually snuff out life. A living tradition must accept a challenge as a test. If it has strong roots and nourishing fruits, it emerges from the test with roots strengthened and fruits ripened.

The great Gaon Saadia (882-942) accepted for Judaism the challenge of Islam and Karaism. Intellectual energies long dormant in Judaism were released and stimulated to activity. Islamic theology forced Saadia to clarify Judaism and to give it philosophic system and expression. His *magnum opus, Beliefs and Opinions,* which wedded reason and revelation, was the fountainhead of a rich flow of philosophic activity over the next five centuries. It not only strengthened Judaism, but is still a major contribution to the formal wisdom of Western man. In response to Karaism's advances in Biblical studies, Saadia felt impelled to prepare philological and Biblical works which were valuable in themselves and served as catalysts for others. Of particular worth was his translation of the Bible into Arabic. With vast erudition and singular insight, he successfully upheld tradition's claim to ideological and practical superiority.

Above all, Saadia's activity demonstrated that Judaism's roots are struck deep beside wells of living waters which nourish and refresh. When Islam's desert sun threatened to parch the roots and when Karaite regression menaced fruit and flower, the Jew drank deep of the living waters of his tradition. With soul refreshed and faith strengthened, he went forth on his journey westward in space and upward in spirit.

UNDER CRESCENT AND CROSS

The movement of Jewish life westward from Babylonia is reflected in a chronicler's historic legend. Four scholars, it is reported, set out from the Academy at Sura to solicit support for it. A shipwreck scattered them, one reaching Egypt, another North Africa, a third, southern France, and the fourth, Spain. Reflected in the legend is the historic fact that centers of Jewish life and learning did rise up in these areas and that scholarly inspiration and guidance came from Babylonia. It is the history of the Jewish people in the Diaspora that hardly had the sun begun to set on one community, than it began to rise for a successor. Some see in this the workings of a benevolent Providence, others attribute it to the remarkable instinct for survival of this people, and its unquenchable will to live.

The emissary who reached Spain in the middle of the tenth century found an already flourishing Jewry. The Moslem rulers permitted worth to outweigh prejudice. Jews of ability were granted the opportunity to rise high in commerce, in the professions, and even in government. Those who found themselves possessed of influence and affluence used both to further religious scholarship and intellectual creativity. The period which followed is justly called "The Golden Age of Spanish Jewry."

The physician-statesman Hasdai ibn Shaprut established and supported academies of learning. Samuel ibn Nagdela was not only the influential advisor of the king of Grenada, but a gifted poet and a noted scholar as well. Abraham ibn Ezra's commentary on the Bible and Isaac Alfasi's work on the Talmud are cornerstones of their respective studies. The poets, Moses ibn Ezra, Solomon ibn Gabirol, and Judah Halevi wrote the only great Hebrew poetry between the days of the psalmists and our own time. The latter two were also philosophers whose influence extended beyond their century and their people. The Jewry of Moorish Spain was a community valued for its contribution to economic life and respected for its cultural achievement.

But religious prejudice was not dead. It lay dormant for years, but could and did rise in spasmodic fury to organize pogroms and decree exile. The finest flowering of Spanish Jewry, Moses ben Maimon, called Maimonides, experienced the wrath of persecution. As a youngster, he was forced to flee his native Cordova, eventually making his home in Egypt. A multi-faceted genius, he was at home in the sciences, in medicine, in philosophy and in Jewish law, and made basic and lasting contributions to each. His systemization of the whole body of Talmudic law is a tour-de-force of scholarship. For the perplexed of his age, he wrote a *Guide,* a work of religious philosophy, "an harmonization . . . of the postulates of reason with the dogmas of faith. It is reason mitigated by faith, and faith regulated by reason." He is the Rabbin Moses one finds quoted with approval and appreciation in medieval Christian philosophical and theological works.

These, and many others, were the heroes who made the age golden. Not men who wielded sword or scepter, but those who took up pen in spiritual battle, and kept the Eternal "enthroned in the praises of Israel."

PERSECUTION AND MARTYRDOM

The Jews of Christian Europe could boast of no Golden Age to parallel that of Moslem Spain. For one, Islamic culture of a thousand years ago was unmatched in quality or quantity. Then again, the Jew was neither invited nor permitted to share the culture of the Christian lands. Truth to tell, Islam's crescent now waned, now waxed, in the freedom and opportunities granted the adherents of the Mother Faith. The Cross was harsher by far. The history of the Jew in medieval Europe is a story of persecution, expulsion, and martyrdom. During the Crusades, community after community was confronted with the choice: the cross or the sword. The mantle of martyrdom was forced upon whole congregations.

The memories of these dread times are retained in the liturgy.

> May the Father of mercies, who dwelleth on high, in His mighty compassion, remember those loving, upright, and blameless ones, the holy congregations, who laid down their lives for the sanctification of the divine name, who were lovely and pleasant in their lives, and in their death were not divided; swifter than eagles, stronger than lions to do the will of their Maker and the desire of their Rock.

The author, who witnessed persecution and pillage, adds a verse grand in its humanity.

> May our God remember them for good with the other righteous of the world.

Even in his moment of anguish, the Jew remembers that among the nations of the world there are the righteous as well as the wicked.

Fiendish accusations were invented to justify persecution. Ritual murder, desecration of the host, poisoning of wells. What plot did not the twisted mind invent to wash the bloody hand!

In the Ghetto

It has been said that "Jewish life is dark without and beautiful within."

The Jew was relegated to the most despised trades and most precarious professions. He was shut up in crowded ghettos. One hand was always on the wanderer's staff. He lived in a world where he was despised and hunted. And in this ugly world of darkness and hatred, he kept the light of learning burning bright, and made his life beautiful in spirit, morality, and compassion.

There were no Dark Ages for European Jewry. Learning flourished under the most adverse circumstances. In a world where reading and writing were arts reserved for the few, education for boys was mandatory. The great Rashi's commentaries on the Bible and Talmud made their teachings available to all the folk. The Jew built no cathedrals, but he did found and maintain academies of higher learning.

The responsibility of one Jew for the welfare of his fellow Jew was a cardinal principle of Jewish life. The poor were aided by organized charities, the bride dowered, the captives ransomed, the dead given proper burial. All were religious duties, carried on with a high sense of concern and dedication.

Nor was life altogether somber. On the Sabbath, the Jew was king in his household, his wife the queen, children, royalty all. Holiday celebrations were a commingling of joy and holiness. The festival of Purim was a special occasion for joy. A literary people produced works of the imagination which piqued, excited, and entertained, and a healthy sense of humor gave perspective and proper proportion to life.

EXPULSION

Country after country, with hardly an exception, made its Jews wandering Jews.

England in 1290.

France throughout the 14th century.

The German states during the 15th.

But the great expulsion was that of Spanish Jewry. The lot of the Jew worsened in Spain as cross supplanted crescent. Riots, forced conversion, economic oppression took their toll. The Holy Inquisition filled the land with the cries of the tortured, whose souls were purified by breaking their bodies on rack and wheel. Martyrs breathed their last in *auto-da-fe* flames.

The remnants of the once great, powerful, and influential Spanish Jewry were ordered out of the lands of their Catholic majesties, Ferdinand and Isabella. They could buy asylum through conversion. But some 100,000, loyal to the faith of their fathers, chose to brave the perils of the wanderer. The last groups left on August 2, 1492, which was the Jewish fast day, Tishah B'Av, commemorating the destruction of the First and Second Temples. In the Jewish consciousness this latter day tragedy was no less a national calamity.

August 2, 1492 was also the day on which Christopher Columbus set sail westward. That his journey led to the discovery of a land which became a refuge and home for a community of this people, unmatched in number in all its history, is one of those ironic turns of fate which dot our history. The faithful, however, say: "The God of History will not be denied."

A descendant of the wanderers, four centuries later in the New World, remembered her forebears. Emma Lazarus wrote:

THE EXODUS (August 3, 1492)

1. The Spanish noon is a blaze of azure fire, and the dusty pilgrims crawl like an endless serpent along treeless plains and bleached high-roads . . .

2. The heavy patriarch, wrinkled as an almond shell, bows painfully upon his staff. The beautiful young mother, ivory pale, well nigh swoons beneath her burden; in her large enfolding arms nestles her sleeping babe, round her knees flock her little ones with bruised and bleeding feet. "Mother, shall we soon be there?" . . .

6. Noble and abject, learned and simple, illustrious and obscure, plod side by side, all brothers now, all merged in one routed army of misfortune.

7. Woe to the straggler who falls by the wayside! No friends shall close his eyes . . .

12. Whither shall they turn? for the West hath cast them out, and the East refuseth to receive.

The exiles and their descendants rebuilt their lives in North Africa, Italy, Turkey, Holland; and were among the earliest settlers in the New World. A goodly number returned to the Holy Land, which soon boasted communities of scholars, poets, and mystics. The scholar-mystic, Joseph Caro, compiled the Code of Law, *Shulchan Arukh,* whose authority and influence have not been superseded.

WHEN WILL THE MESSIAH COME?

The persecutions and expulsions in Western Europe drove many Jews eastward to a friendly welcome in the Kingdom of Poland. Sometime during the eighth century a nation, in what is now Southern Russia, the Khazars, had adopted Judaism. When the kingdom was overrun by the Tartars some five centuries later, many remained Jews and moved westward across Russia to Poland. A third group came from the Eastern Roman or Byzantine Empire.

Enlightened kings of Poland extended to them opportunities in commerce and trade. Having established themselves economically, the Jews of Poland directed their energies to matters of the spirit, and a flourishing scholarly culture emerged. Study of the Talmud was at the center of intellectual enterprise. The synagogues became academies of learning. Illiteracy was almost unknown, and an amazing number were scholars of the first order. Life was wholly under the domain of Jewish law. Early 17th century Polish Jewry was a total religious civilization.

Jacob enthroned the book, but Esau wielded the sword. In the middle of the century a Cossack rebellion swept across the Ukraine into Poland. Jewish history remembers it as "the calamities of '48-'49." Communities were wiped out, countless Jews put to the sword. A chronicler sums it up in noble words:

> We are ashamed to write down all that the Cossacks and Tartars did unto the Jews, lest we disgrace the species man who is created in the image of God.

When will the Messiah come?

Rabbi Johanan taught:

> The Messiah will come when the eyes of men will grow dim
> with weeping and sighing: when afflictions will multiply and
> evil decree will follow evil decree.

To the Jew of mid-17th-century Europe, the days of the
Messiah were at hand. Their number had dwindled to less
than one million. Crescent, cross, and sword had reaped their
victory. Only the miraculous coming of the Anointed One
could save God's people. The practical mystics, the Cabbalists,
had even set the year of his coming—1648.

In that year a young visionary of the Turkish city of Smyrna,
Sabbetai Zvi, announced himself the Messiah. Others had done
so before him, but none had fired the imagination nor inspired
belief as did he. The wretched times had implanted in many
people the will to believe the miraculous. His captivating personality and his gift for leadership combined with incidents in
his life, real and imagined, to convince the skeptic. Soon he was
hailed the Messiah throughout the Jewish world. Whole communities of Jews made ready to follow him to the Holy Land.

A modern scholar muses:

> It is curious . . . that the same race which had been critical
> over a Moses should have been credulous over a Sabbetai Zvi.

Desperation fostered credulity. A people's plight gave birth
to belief—bizarre as it was.

Great was the shock when the erstwhile Messiah accepted
the green turban of Moslem conversion to save his life. Even
so some of his followers continued to believe in him, creating
fanciful excuses and explanations. But for the multitude disillusionment was added to despair. They turned again for
leadership to the sober scholars who had cautioned and warned
them.

When will the Messiah come?

"Today, if ye hearken to His voice," taught R. Simeon bar Yohai.

The people turned to hearken to His voice in study and through obedience to His Law.

INTO THE MODERN WORLD

Destruction and disillusionment often lead to despair. But not for Israel. Hardships had been met and overcome in the past. The people and its faith which contributed so much to humanity in the past "has not yet played out its part, and, therefore, may not perish." The biblical admonition "Choose life!" was accepted as a national command.

How does a people "choose life"? The 18th century witnessed the acting out of three answers, each put forth and symbolized by a towering spiritual personality.

THE MIND

In the city of Vilna, called "The Jerusalem of Lithuania," a giant of intellect sat in a humble room, studying and writing. Through example and challenge, he inspired generations of Jews to live out Judaism's ancient doctrine: study is the highest pursuit of man.

Even during Europe's Dark Ages, when the Jew suffered oppression and persecution, his lust for learning did not abate. The English historian Lecky attests:

> While those around them were grovelling in the darkness of besotten ignorance . . . the Jews were still pursuing the path of knowledge, amassing learning and stimulating progress with the same unflinching constancy that they manifested in their faith.

Elijah, son of Abraham, called the Gaon of Vilna, was a spiritual force whose influence transcended his life and deeds. A master of every branch of Jewish learning, he became the symbol of the scholar *par excellence*. Academies of higher learning sprang up as monuments to his spirit and influence. He was equally celebrated in scholars' zeal and in mothers' lullabies. The most desirable son-in-law was the promising scholar, for the communities were dominated by an aristocracy of the learned. The Jewry of northeast Europe made the admonition "thou shalt study diligently day and night" the chief of commandments.

Immersion in the sacred texts insulated the Jew against the hostility of the world without. Study was the balm that healed the wounds of political oppression, social ostracism, and economic exploitation. Learning not only restored life; it was life itself. This single-minded preoccupation with learning produced, in the centuries that followed, men of prodigious scholarly attainment, who helped illumine man's mind and uplift his spirit.

The Heart

But what of the people not blessed with keenness of mind, whose love for God was great and whose devotion to Judaism strong? Any aristocracy is tainted by arrogance, even the aristocracy of the learned. In truth, the Talmudic scholar and student looked down upon the unlearned and untutored. But even these were descendants of prophets, sages and martyrs, who revered the Law and longed for communion with God. Does God really prefer the knowledge of the scholar to the sincere piety of the common folk? The Book, to be sure, can be the bridge to God, but when the bridge remains uncrossed it becomes a barrier. Study is the language of the mind, the language of the heart is prayer. Did not the sages teach that "God desires the heart"!

It may be that among the prayers there was an unvoiced supplication for a leader who would give expression and system to the sentiments and yearnings of the folk. If so, their prayers were answered in the person of Israel, called Baal

Shem Tov (Master of the Good Name). He lived and taught in southern Poland, till his death in 1760.

What were his teachings?

He was not a scholar and philosopher, and left no writings. He was a folk teacher and revivalist, expounding his message in parable, homily, and tale. But he effected a spiritual revolution. God is everywhere, in everything, he and his disciples taught. He is as accessible to the ignorant as to the learned, to the sinner as to the saint. "Every man must devote all his capabilities to the service of God, for all things are intended to serve God." Man is to yearn for Him, and cleave to Him. God is to be served in joy and with enthusiasm, with an outpouring of the spirit in song and dance. Prayer is the royal road to the Heavenly Father. The Father's concern is for all His children, His love even for the most lowly. He delights in the saint and awaits the repentance of the sinner. He is a loving Father whose hand is stretched forth to every child who longs to grasp it.

For a people recalling a recent foe that showed no mercy and a recent Messiah who was a deceiver, this blend of mysticism and optimism held great attraction. The disciples of Baal Shem Tov won thousands upon thousands of *hassidim* (pious ones) to his banner. The movement generated tremendous religious enthusiasm and spirit, and saw the people through difficult periods. In time it also degenerated into substituting form for substance and freezing the free-flowing creative spirit which it had liberated. But its spiritual legacy of insight into the relationship of God and man, man and fellow-man, and its teachings about prayer, compassion, and faith, are of lasting value. They have been introduced to a wide audience in our century through the writings of Martin Buber, Abraham Joshua Heschel, and others.

THE OPEN DOOR

The world of Eastern Europe was hostile to the Jew, so he turned his gaze inward to his tradition and upward to God.

In Western Europe, the 18th century was the period of Enlightenment. "Toleration" was a word much in vogue, and Jews began to dare hope for civic rights and an acceptance which they had never enjoyed in any European country. Political emancipation had to be preceded by integration of the Jew into the culture of the land. It was desirable that the cultured neighbor learn about and respect Judaism, and the Jew had to make his contribution to the nascent national culture. In short, the door between the Jewish community and the outside world, which had remained shut these many centuries, had to be opened.

In 1743, a young hunchbacked Jew stood before the Rosenthal gate in Berlin, begging entry into the city of Frederick the Great. His stated business: "To study!" For the next forty-three years Moses Mendelssohn studied. But far more than he studied, he taught. He taught the residents of the capital city of Prussia to admire German culture, and respect their native philosophers and men of letters. From his translation of the Pentateuch into German, the Jews of middle-Europe learned the German language. Knowledge of the language was the key which opened the door to the outside world. The acceptance of Mendelssohn as a leader of German cultural renaissance encouraged many brilliant and talented young Jews to enter through the opened door. They found, however, that the ticket of admission into academic life and the world of letters was a baptismal certificate. For many the open door led out of the house of Judaism. But there were many more, equally gifted but stronger in character, who used the new found tools of language and research to effect a renaissance of Jewish learning. The century which followed was rich in cultural creativity and religious ferment.

Mendelssohn was as much admired for his soul as for his mind. The nobility of his character moved men of good will to advocate political rights for the Jews. But prejudice dies hard, and many decades were to elapse before such rights were extended to German Jewry.

The French Revolution, with its Declaration of the Rights of Man, heralded freedom and justice for the Jews of Europe. Napoleon, son of the revolution, extended citizenship to the Jews in the lands of his conquests. Napoleon, the emperor, found it to be good imperial policy as well. The reaction which set in after the final defeat of Napoleon at Waterloo erased most of the rights granted. But the Jews of Western Europe, having tasted freedom, waged a valiant battle to preserve it, and where denied, to regain it. As the forces of light beat back the forces of darkness on the European continent, the rays of the rising sun shone on the Jews as well.

SANCTUARY AND HOME

The first country to extend full political and civic rights to its Jewish inhabitants was the United States of America.

George Washington wrote to the Jews of Newport, Rhode Island:

> The citizens of the United States of America have a right to applaud themselves for having given to mankind examples of an enlarged and liberal policy, a policy worthy of imitation. All possess alike liberty of conscience and immunities of citizenship.

The Jews of America were aware of their unique good fortune. The Rev. Gershom Mendes Seixas of New York expressed it in a sermon delivered on May 9, 1798:

> It hath pleased God to have established us in this country where we possess every advantage that other citizens of these states enjoy.

In September 1654, twenty-three Jewish men, women, and children sought sanctuary in New Amsterdam, fleeing from the Inquisition which had established itself in South America. In their wake, families and individuals made their home in the colonies of North America. The twenty-five hundred Jews who lived there during the Revolution participated in the conflict and hailed the Declaration and Constitution which extended to them freedom and equality. Their descendants and new immigrants became integrated in the economic and cultural life of the country, and were looked upon as valued citizens.

Haym Salomon, devout Jew and ardent patriot, helped in some measure to finance the Revolutionary War. Mordecai Manuel Noah was a noted playwright, editor, and political figure during the first half of the 19th century. Judah Touro of New Orleans was the first of an imposing group of Jewish philanthropists, and Commodore Uriah P. Levy was largely responsible for the abolition of flogging in the United States Navy. A sonnet by Emma Lazarus is inscribed on the base of the Statue of Liberty.

The Jews of the United States used their freedom widely and fully in defense of their faith, in support of the American institutions of separation of church and state and equality of opportunity, and in concern for the welfare of their brethren in faith less fortunately situated. A blood accusation in Damascus in 1840, the kidnaping and conversion of the boy Edgar Mortara in the Papal States in 1858, hunger in Morocco, need in Palestine, brought forth protest or aid from the young, small, but free and vigorous community.

An ever-increasing number of Jews sought sanctuary and made their home in the United States. They brought with them a yearning for freedom and opportunity and a variety of economic skill, cultural attainments, and religious views. The variety made for color and ferment. But above the diversity reigned the unity of common historic memories, shared religious commitments, and mutual concern for fellow Jews. Though cultural and religious life left much to be desired, American Jewry then, as always, excelled in the establishment and maintenance of institutions of social welfare, and in the scope of philanthropic endeavor. Orphanages, homes for the aged, free loan societies, and organized charities answered the needs of an immigrant population, and served as challenge and models for the general community.

In the last two decades of the 19th and the first two of the 20th centuries, Jewish immigration, which had been numbered in the thousands, rose to the hundreds of thousands. This dramatic increase was the result of anti-Jewish riots and repressive laws which aimed at the economic strangulation of Russian Jewry. The great Bear of the East had slumbered on, untouched by the spirit of liberality and enlightenment which lifted the West out of the Middle Ages. The plight of Russian Jewry, the world's largest Jewish community, was precarious. Emigration was not only Jewish hope, but also government policy. The Jews of Russia turned their eyes westward across the Atlantic to the new land of promise. But there were some who looked eastward to the ancient Promised Land.

ON TO ZION

The Jew had never forgotten Zion. For eighteen hundred years he had prayed for its restoration. In every century, groups of Jews returned to the Holy Land. Emissaries from these settlers circled the earth and were a living bridge which connected the communities of the Diaspora with that of Palestine. Many were there who dreamed of Redemption and yearned for Return. Mordecai Manuel Noah proclaimed in 1824:

> We will return to Zion as we went forth, bringing back the faith we carried away with us.

In the second half of the 19th century perceptive Jews recognized that liberalism had not erased anti-Semitism. Nationalism was then a strengthening, liberating force. Prayers and longing became political program.

In Germany, the spiritual leader Zechariah Frankel argued:

> A people without a center or a government of its own can never attain to honor among the nations of the world.

Just a century ago the disillusioned socialist Moses Hess challenged:

> March forward, Jews of all lands!
> The ancient fatherland of yours is calling you . . .

In Russia, Leon Pinsker declared:

> In order that we may not be compelled to wander from one exile to another, we must have a place of refuge, a rallying point of our own.

Desire was implemented by the practical work of colonization. Dedicated young Jews called *halutzim* (pioneers) established agricultural colonies in Palestine. They redeemed the land, drained the swamps, and began to build a society which would be the fulfilment of the prophetic ideals of social justice. "Lovers of Zion" organizations were established in other Jewish communities as well, to support the work of the *halutzim* and enlarge upon it.

What was needed was a leader who could fire the imagination and arouse the enthusiasm of world Jewry, so that scattered clubs of zealots could be transformed into a mass movement. The leader was Theodor Herzl, a Viennese journalist whose true vocation was leadership and whose mission was Zionism. Shocked by the virulent anti-Semitism which he encountered in the "enlightened" countries of Western Europe, most particularly as manifested in the Dreyfus case in France, he concluded:

> The Jews have but one way of saving themselves—a return to their own people and an emigration to their own land.

To Herzl, return and rebuilding would be not only a solution to "the Jewish problem," but also:

> The world will be freer by our liberty, richer by our wealth, greater by our greatness.

The great Zionist Congress which he convened in Basle, Switzerland in 1897 declared:

Zionism aims to create for the Jewish people a publicly recognized and legally secured home in Palestine.

The east European Zionists, who were then effecting a great Hebraic cultural renaissance, saw in Zionism a promise more than political. Their spokesman, Ahad Ha-am, declared:

In Palestine we can and should found for ourselves a spiritual center of our nationality.

Pioneers went up to the Land, established cooperative colonies, drained swamps, planted trees, made the ancient holy tongue, Hebrew, a living language, and set high examples of selflessness and sacrifice. The world looked on with amazement, and then with approval. As World War I was coming to an end Great Britain issued the Balfour Declaration, which stated:

His Majesty's Government views with favor the establishment in Palestine of a national home for the Jewish people . . .

The world added its agreement through acceptance of the Declaration by the League of Nations.

The years which followed the War "to make the world safe for democracy" saw the rise of dictatorships. The most vicious of the tyrants, Hitler, singled out the Jewish people as his chief enemy. Restrictive legislation and government-inspired persecution on a scale hitherto unknown doomed the once proud and creative German Jewry. The Jewish community which constituted 1% of Germany's population had given it 30% of its Nobel Prize winners.

At the outbreak of World War II, there were in the world some seventeen million Jews. Of these, ten million lived in Europe. At war's end there remained in Europe fewer than four million Jews. Over six million men, women and children, unarmed civilians, were ruthlessly murdered by German armies and their civilian co-workers. Unspeakable tortures were visited upon the innocent in concentration camps and ghettos. Man, having descended, sank to the depths of degradation. In specially constructed gas chambers, millions were scientifically put to death, their bodies turned to ashes in giant crematoria.

These things do I remember and my soul I pour forth.
How the arrogant have devoured my people.

Living ghosts were rescued from death camps to haunt the post-war world.

On the 29th of November, 1947, the United Nations General Assembly called for establishment of a Jewish State in Palestine. It thus gave international sanction and approval to a hounded and harried people to seek security, well-being, and self-fulfilment in its ancestral homeland. The Jewish community of Palestine was ready for statehood, and its leaders proclaimed the establishment of the State of Israel on May 14, 1948. The neighboring Arab states despatched their armies to crush the new state. Men and women, possessed of the courage given only to those who stand in defense of home and family, beat back the enemy and secured the boundaries of their new homeland. The war over, the defenders turned to an equally heroic enterprise of rescue and rehabilitation.

The Declaration of Statehood announced:

The State of Israel will be open for Jewish immigration and for the ingathering of the exiles; it will foster the development of the country for the benefit of all the inhabitants; it will be based on freedom, justice and peace as envisaged by the prophets of Israel . . .

Who were the exiles to be ingathered? Thousands upon thousands of European Jews, alumni of the Nazi concentration camps, marked for the gas chambers when the victorious allies overran Germany; the inhabitants of the mellahs of North Africa and the ghettos of the Arab countries of the Near East, eking out a desperate existence with few rights and less hope. In the first thirteen years of Israel's statehood a community of 650,000 gave sanctuary and home, new life and new hope to over 1,000,000 immigrants. This constituted an act of compassion unprecedented and unmatched in the history of man's concern for fellow man.

The ideals of the prophets of Israel are finding fulfilment in the new state through legislation, which fosters economic justice and social equality, and through institutions which care for the health and well-being of all the citizenry.

Isaiah of Jerusalem proclaimed that "out of Zion shall go forth the Law." His namesake in Babylonian exile challenged the people to its national destiny—to be "a light unto the nations." This little democracy, beset by its own internal problems of caring for so vast a population of newcomers, and threatened by hostile neighbors, nevertheless is responding to the call of destiny. As its contribution to world peace and well-being, it has undertaken an ambitious program of sharing with the emergent nations of Africa and Asia its own experiences in all fields of endeavor. A significant number of governmental leaders and technical experts from these new states come to Israel to study its governmental structure, its economic legislation and enterprises, its programs of social service, and its educational system. Teams of Israeli experts have gone forth to these countries to teach agricultural techniques, hygienic care, and social and communal organization.

Israel is teaching, through its experience and example, how a new nation can establish inner security, economic stability, and social well-being in freedom and democracy.

"A COMMUNITY BLESSED"

In the enterprise of rescue and rehabilitation, Israel has had a generous and dedicated partner. During the fifteen post-war years, the five and one-half million Jews of the United States contributed almost one and one-quarter billion dollars to aid their brethren overseas—a philanthropic endeavor unmatched in scope and unparalleled in achievement.

This ambitious enterprise did much for the displaced and the despised. It also brought together in common cause the various elements of the community. Mutuality of interest united groups differing in political outlook, economic status, and religious commitment. In the unity, however, diversity persists. Unity there is in civic concern and philanthropic effort; diversity in religious views and affiliation.

What is the nature of this community marked by civic unity and religious diversity?

A Jewish communal leader recently wrote:

> Jews are, first and enduringly, a *religious* community . . . The primacy of religion, with its organized institutions and rituals, is fundamental to the term "Jew" and to a continuing Jewish community.

The great national Jewish organizations whose program is the strengthening of democracy, the enhancement of social justice, and the extension of civil rights; the network of institutions caring for the aged and the sick; the institutions of learning and organs of culture are all expressions of the Jewish spirit and answers to its religious mandate. Judaism, as we shall see, is as wide as life itself. Its purpose is the enhancement of life, and all institutions which foster that purpose are its legitimate manifestations.

During the twentieth century there have been three expressions of the Jewish religion in America, the Orthodox, the Conservative, and the Reform. Each has created its ideology and literature, and each has institutionalized its being in theological seminaries, rabbinic bodies, and congregational associations.

Orthodoxy clings to the entirety of Jewish tradition. It teaches that the totality of Jewish religious tradition, the Bible, the Talmud, and the Commentaries, "was given by God Himself to Moses on Mount Sinai to be delivered to the Jews and to be observed by them forever." Scrupulous observance of the Jewish Law, as it has come down from generation to generation, is demanded. Interpretation and application of the law is the prerogative of the leading rabbinic scholars of a generation. Great emphasis is placed on the study of traditional texts.

Its leading schools are the Isaac Elchanan Theological Seminary and Yeshiva University in New York, and the Hebrew Theological College in Chicago. Orthodoxy has experienced a revival in the post-war years.

The Reform Movement in Judaism originated in Germany, but had its fullest development in the United States. Its leading spokesman, Abraham Geiger, declared:

> Judaism is not a finished tale. There is much in its present form that must be changed or abolished.

Much was changed and abolished. Reform Judaism feels itself bound only by the ethical teachings of Judaism, not by its ritual laws and traditions. Individual rabbis and congregations are free to accept or reject Jewish rituals and laws as they see fit. There is full freedom for experimentation and improvisation. Classic Reform, stressing the universalistic aspects of Judaism, was strongly anti-Zionist, and all but dispensed with the Hebrew language in its temples and schools.

Of late there has been a reemphasis on tradition in the ranks of the Reform. Ceremonies and ritual have been reintroduced to temple and home; there is a renewed respect for Jewish law and wider use of the Hebrew language.

The Hebrew Union College-Jewish Institute of Religion in Cincinnati and New York trains the Reform rabbinate.

The spiritual fountainhead of Conservative Judaism is the Jewish Theological Seminary of America.

Dr. Robert Gordis, professor at the Jewish Theological Seminary and past president of the Rabbinical Assembly, states:

> . . . the basic postulates of Conservative Judaism . . . (are) the maintenance of the twin principles of authority and development in Jewish law . . . together with the emphasis on the worldwide peoplehood of Israel . . .

According to another spokesman, Rabbi Milton Steinberg,

> Conservative Judaism . . . consists largely in attempting to strike a "happy medium" between the two extremes, in the effort to hold on to as much of the tradition as is tenable and

to make such adjustments in Jewish life and thought as circumstances forcibly compel.

The three movements are nominally united in the Synagogue Council of America. Beyond organizational cooperation, there is a basic unity through shared heritage, commitment, and aspirations. The conclusion of Philip M. Klutznick, able national leader and perceptive student of Jewish life, is instructive:

> Each group accepts the omniscience and eternity of God; each adheres to a distinctively Judaic concept of moral law with its emphasis on the special expression of ethical behavior, love, and social justice; each respects learning and tradition; each follows a recognizable similar form of group worship and ritual; each is imbued with a sense of Jewish history. The significant truth is that the theological concepts that divide Judaism are far less meaningful than the living realities by which Jews are united in common faith.

As the seventh decade of the twentieth century opened there were some twelve million Jews in the world. The two and one-half million behind the Iron Curtain are being crushed spiritually. Their future as Jews is bleak indeed, although one hears now and again of an upsurge of religious feeling in the face of official disapproval and worse. Of the once numerically great, culturally creative, and spiritually exalted European Jewry, only a handful remains to tend the graveyard which the continent became under Nazi domination.

The Jewries of England, South America, South Africa and Australia are in the throes of cultural and religious ferment which many observers view with optimism. The almost two million Jews of Israel constitute a socially vibrant and spiritually zealous community.

By far the largest Jewish community is that of the United States. Its members are well-integrated in every aspect of American life. They give leadership to certain industries, and hold positions of honor and responsibilty in public life. Of particular significance has been their participation in the professions, scholarship, literature, and the arts. As a community, the Jews of the United States have excelled in their institutions for physical and social welfare, and in their organizations for the preservation and enhancement of the democratic spirit.

The Jew is free and feels secure in America, where he sought sanctuary and found a home. His religion is accorded recognition as one of "the three great faiths of America." In turn, his institutions of higher learning have contributed significantly to the spiritual life of this land.

Of late there has been an ever-increasing concern for scholarly and cultural creativity, a widening and deepening interest in the life of the spirit, and an intensification of religious education among children and adults.

The vision of the Prophet of the Exile remains for the Jewish people of this generation both challenge and goal:

> And marked will be their seed among the nations, and their offspring among the peoples. Everyone that will see them will point to them as being a community blessed by the Lord.

CHARIOT AND MENORAH

Among the imposing ruins of Rome is the Arch of Titus. It was erected by order of the Roman Senate to celebrate the triumphant return of Titus in the year 70 from his military conquest of Jerusalem and his destruction of the Temple.

A frieze on the arch portrays the victory procession. The Roman conquerors are riding in chariots. Judean captives carry the great Menorah, the candelabrum which illumined the Temple.

Today descendants of the vanquished who carried the Menorah on their shoulders visit Rome, see the arch, and gaze upon the frieze. Many are on their way to visit the new State of Israel and the revived Jerusalem.

The writer of these lines did so in 1954. As he stood before the arch, the words of the prophet Zechariah came to him:

Not by might, nor by power, but by My spirit, saith the Lord of Hosts.

And he thought: Victory is not to those who ride in chariots, but to those who carry the Menorah. This is the story of my people!

2

THE LORD,
THE LORD...

We comprehend only that He exists, not His essence.

MAIMONIDES

The rav (Rabbi Shneur Zalman of Ladi) asked a disciple who had just entered his room:
"Moshe, what do we mean when we say 'God'?"
The disciple was silent. The rav asked him a second and a third time. Then he said:
"Why are you silent?"
"Because I do not know."
"Do you think I know?" said the rav.
"But I must say it, for it is so, and therefore I must say it: He is definitely there, and except for him nothing is definitely there—and this is He."

MARTIN BUBER
Tales of the Hassidim

THE CREATOR WHO IS ONE

How does man know God?

The philosopher contemplates the First Cause, the Prime Mover, the Mind of Cosmos.

The mystic sees Him in every fragment of creation and feels His presence with every fibre of his being.

The Jew?

Moses prayed:

"If I have found favor in Thy sight, show me now Thy ways, that I may know Thee."

We know God through His works.

Rabbi Abba ben Memel taught:

The Holy One, Blessed be He, said to Moses: You want to know My name? My name is according to My work.

God is introduced to man in the first verse of the Bible.

In the beginning God created the heaven and the earth.

A grand declaration, majestic in its simplicity and strength. No pleading, no argument, no qualification, but the sober measured statement that there is One God, the Creator of all.

Every affirmation is also a negation. Modern man, reading the Bible's opening sentence, views it as a denial of atheism and as a rejection of the notion that the world "just happened." The ancient world knew no atheists. Gods there were aplenty, a pantheon diverse and divided. Man believed the world to be eternal, the gods creatures of creation.

The Jewish declaration of faith—"Hear O Israel, the Lord is our God, the Lord is one"—is both an assertion and a refutation. To paganism it said: God is one, and not many. To Zoroastrianism it proclaimed that God is not two. It denied the Christian concept of a trinity.

Throughout its history, Judaism has sternly insisted on the oneness of God, undivided and undiminished. Martyrs proclaimed His unity and returned their souls with "the Lord our God, the Lord is one" upon their lips.

Why the insistence on God's unity?

To the Jew "God is one" is not so much a theologic truth or philosophic conclusion as it is a religious teaching. It proclaims his view of the universe and of his place in it; it expresses his concept of humanity and of the relationship of man to man.

What does "God is one" mean?

God is one means that the universe is one. Harmony and order mark the physical world. Order and harmony provide for man the basis for an optimistic faith. The cosmos into which he has been cast is orderly and can be made friendly. Man is not buffeted about by capricious physical forces perilous in their undependability. The refrain which runs through the epic of creation, "And God saw that it was good"—is the poetic celebration of a harmonious and friendly universe.

God is one tells man that the God who fashioned the universe created him, placed him in it, and charged him to "replenish the earth and subdue it." The Creator has given His creation as a gift to His creature, man, "to work it and to guard it." God granted man a greater gift still: the knowledge that the earth will respond to man's care, that nature can be tamed by man's concern.

One God means one humanity. How better to state that all men are brothers and sisters than to proclaim, as did the prophet Malachi: "Have we not all one Father, hath not one God created us!"?

One God created us. The greatest Jewish philosopher and legal authority of the Middle Ages, Moses Maimonides, taught:

> The fundamental of all fundamentals and the pillar of all forms of knowledge is the realization that there is a First Being who brought all existing things into being.

God the Creator is neither proven nor argued in the Bible. His existence is taken for granted, even as His work is seen and experienced. We cannot know His being. A sage wisely explained "If I would know Him, I would be He." We can only glimpse His existence and reality in His works and express it in analogy. Throughout the ages men of great faith have seen Him in all aspects of creation.

At the birth of our faith, Moses implored: "Show me Thy ways."

Eighteen centuries ago the great Rabbi Akiba, chief architect of rabbinic Judaism, argued:

> As a house implies a builder, a dress a weaver, a door a carpenter, so the world proclaims God, its Creator.

A millennium later, Abba Mari proclaimed:

> We need no ladders to the sky, we need only . . . observe the structure and functions of man's bodily organs . . . to know that the Creator exists.

In our own day, the rationalist Joshua Loth Liebman wrote:

> ". . . we come upon Him at work in the majesty of nature and the fruitfulness of mind, in the laws of atoms and the goals of men."

The mystic Abraham Joshua Heschel questions: "If there were no God, then who lit the wonder before our eyes and the wonder of our eyes?"

Except as a shield to defend itself against the intellectual onslaught of other faiths, Judaism has dealt little with theology, which a contemporary rabbi calls "that madness gone systematic which tries to crowd God's fullness into a formula and a system." Judaism is not so much concerned with establishing that God exists or with ascribing attributes to Him, as with the question: "What are the practical consequences of belief in God?"

The principal purpose of Jewish religious teaching is to regulate conduct. The theoretical is but a preface to the practical. Beliefs are premises not conclusions. Conclusions are not theological concepts, but moral teachings. The final question is not, "What shall I therefore believe?" but "How must I therefore act?"

Thus, in considering the attributes of God, those which lend themselves to practical application are the desirable ones for discussion. The fruitful and valued discussion is the one whose conclusions become the cornerstones and foundation of the ethical system which is the heart of this faith.

THE JUDGE WHO IS RIGHTEOUS

Rabbi Israel Salanter, leader of a moralist movement in the 19th century, admonished:

> "Faith in the existence of God is of small value in true religion, if it is not supplemented by the belief that God is just . . ."

God is not the cosmic watchmaker, who fashioned the clock, wound it, and sent it out of his shop. He is rather the King-Judge, giver of the law and its enforcer, guiding His people to know and abide by the law. He is the guarantor of the moral law, whose basic principle is justice. God, through prophet and saint, urges his children to choose the good life, but all too often they are led astray by lust and laziness. Those who stray and reject earn chastisement. The Righteous Judge chastises to correct. His rod and wrath are for repentance and rehabilitation. He can do no other, for He Himself, as it were, is bound by His own law of justice.

The cities of Sodom and Gomorrah were filled with sin and wickedness. They had condemned themselves to destruction. Abraham, attempting to save the inhabitants, appealed to God's justice. How could He destroy the righteous with the wicked? "Shall not the judge of all the earth do justly?" God is just and rules the world in justice. The preachment of the prophets was not that God is and man must believe, but that God is just and so man must be.

Each holy day celebrates an attribute of the Holy One. Passover speaks of God as the liberating force in history; Shavuot proclaims Him the Lawgiver; Sukkot is a festival of thanksgiving to God the Provider; the High Holy Days celebrate God as the Righteous Judge. The world and man stand at the bar of justice. Even as God judges man, so man is to judge himself. From the attribute of Righteous Judge, flows the uplifting enterprise of spiritual stock taking, and with it, introspection and contrition, confession and forgiveness, realization and resolve, and humility.

THE FATHER WHO IS MERCIFUL

Would a stern judge have permitted Abraham to challenge the court's integrity? Hardly! As we read Abraham's plea for the condemned cities, we sense the judge desirous of, almost anxious for, Abraham's success. God is not only a righteous Judge; He is also, or above all, a merciful Father.

There is a noble tradition which teaches that the world was created through justice, but is maintained by mercy. Had mercy not been added to justice, the world long since would have condemned itself to deserved destruction.

God demands justice. "Justice, justice shalt thou pursue." Man pleads for mercy, "Our Father, merciful Father." His demand gives us purpose; our plea gives us hope.

The Bible knows the Father's mercy and gives it concrete expression and social application in such laws as this:

> If thou shalt take thy neighbor's raiment in pledge, thou shalt deliver it unto him when the sun goeth down. For it is his only covering, it is his raiment for his skin: wherein shall he sleep? and it shall come to pass, when he crieth unto me, that I will hear him, for I am gracious.

Later the rabbis of the Midrash celebrated God's mercy in more poetic concept and language:

God feels pain each time a man suffers. When the blood of man is spilt, be it even an impious man, God groans and feels the very wounds by which one of his children was wounded.

For whom does a merciful father show concern?

Seest thou a wicked man persecuting a wicked, now that God is with the persecuted; a righteous man persecuting a righteous, God is with the persecuted. Even when the righteous persecute the wicked, by the very fact of their perescution, God is with the persecuted.

THE VALLEY OF THE DARK SHADOW

The Psalmist sang:

Yea, though I walk through the valley of the shadow of death, I will fear no evil.

God's good earth is often a valley of the dark shadow, and evil flourishes. Sickness and suffering, poverty and death, who can escape them? The Book of Job posits the question in all its poignance and pertinence: "Why do the righteous suffer?"

There are those who escape the problem by denying the reality of pain and poverty, even of death itself. Others proclaim affliction to be just punishment for sin. There are some who cry out in their anguish and despair, "there is neither justice nor Judge!"

Judaism rejects these easy solutions. In humbleness it admits that there are things beyond man's knowledge or understanding. Rabbi Jannai taught in the *Ethics of the Fathers:*

To explain the relative peace of the wicked and suffering of the righteous is beyond us.

Meaning there must be, though we cannot fathom it. This world is not the cruel jest of a capricious Creator.

Do we then ignore the shadows and the gloom they cast? Not at all!

We accept death as the price man pays for living. Natural calamities are beyond our ken. But disease is a challenge to our intellect and ingenuity. Poverty is an affliction which tests the heart of mankind. Warfare is our failure to curb our lust for pelf or power. And because humanity is one, the weak and the innocent are most exposed and susceptible to suffering, even as the weakened part of the human body is afflicted by infection when the body is exposed to disease. "Suffering is not an absolute evil; it educates, it purifies, it can be an instrument of divine love," wrote Rabbi Joseph H. Hertz.

What to do in the face of wickedness and evil?

The Prophets taught: Reveal it! Renounce it! Reject it! Resist it! Remove it!

Rabbi Tarfon was wont to say:

> It is not thy duty to complete the work.
> But neither art thou free to desist from it.

And in the end, when all the questions have been exhausted, and the answers, brilliant, clever, and ingenious, have not satisfied the questing mind, nor eased the aching heart, Job's words remain: "Shall we receive good at the hand of God, and shall we not also receive evil?"

A TRIO OF THEOLOGIANS

The twentieth century has not been bereft of Jewish theologians. Three have had most influence.

One was a product of East European Jewish piety and scholarship and became the Chief Rabbi of Palestine, Abraham Isaac Kuk.

The second, a fine flowering of European religious thought, now at the Hebrew University in Jerusalem and a major in-

fluence on European and American religious thought, is
Martin Buber.

The third would be loath to term himself a theologian: an
American rabbi, professor at the Jewish Theological Seminary,
influenced by James and Dewey, Mordecai M. Kaplan.

What do they say of God?

Dr. Mordecai M. Kaplan writes:

What is God?

We suggest that God be thought of as the cosmic process that
makes for man's salvation.

What is belief in God?

. . . belief in God is belief in the existence of a Power con-
ducive to salvation which is the fulfillment of human destiny.

How does man become aware of God?

By the same token that man becomes aware of himself as a
person engaged in a struggle against dangers and difficulties,
he also becomes aware of the help of a Power or Powers to
conquer obstacles. That awareness finds expression in ideas.
What is most distinctive about himself as a person is termed
"soul," and what is most distinctive about the Power or
Powers upon whom he depends is termed "God."

Rabbi Abraham Isaac Kuk is the mystic:

God:

The essence of our knowledge of the Deity is this: that He is
One, the Creator and the Revealer of Commandments. And
all the varied faculties of the spirit are only so many aids to
the solution and the detailed description of this knowledge:
their purpose is to clarify it and present it in a form that will
be at once the most ideal, noble, rational, simple and exalted.

The nearness of God:

And life is so joyous, so sacred, so filled with the majesty of
the name of the Lord. You long to express His name (essence), to interpret the exalted light. You are filled with an
intense thirst, pleasing in the extreme, to fill your mouth with
praise of the God of gods.

Trust in God:

Every spirit is endowed with sweet hope. Trust in God . . . fills all . . . The splendid determination to be uplifted above all epochs of time in order to cleave to the value and splendor of eternity suffuses all things . . .

Professor Martin Buber taught the world how to meet God.

I and *Thou* . . .

All real living is meeting.
The relation to the *Thou* is direct. No system of ideas, no fore-knowledge, and no fancy intervene between *I* and *Thou*.

Through the *Thou* a man becomes *I*.
The *Thou* confronts me. But I step into direct relation with it. Hence the relation means being chosen and choosing . . .

. . . To step into pure relation is not to disregard everything but to see everything in the *Thou;* not to renounce the world but to establish it on a true basis . . . to eliminate or leave behind nothing at all, to include the whole world in the *Thou,* to give the world its due and its truth, to include nothing beside God but everything in Him—this is full and complete relation.

Men do not find God if they stay in the world. They do not find Him if they leave the world. He who goes out with his whole being to meet his *Thou,* and carries to it all being that is in the world, finds Him who cannot be sought.

God cannot be inferred in anything—in nature, say, as its author, or in history, as its master . . . Something else is not "given" and God then elicited from it; but God is the Being that is directly, most nearly, and lastingly, over against us, that may properly only be addressed, not expressed. That which reveals is that which reveals. That which is, *is,* and nothing more. The eternal source of strength streams, the eternal contacts persist, the eternal voice sounds forth and nothing more.

A trio of twentieth century Jewish theologians. How different their roads to God! Pragmatism and naturalism are the way of one. The second gropes for God in mystic exultation. The third goes forth to meet Him in existential confrontation.

As it is now, so it has always been. Judaism has always given the widest latitude for theologic speculation. And yet, for all their varied ways, they travel together. The heritage which impelled them to speak of and to God and gave them the language to do so, unites them. They are sons of the same people, from whom, for whom, and to whom they speak. And in speaking of God, they raise aloft the banner of this people, upon which is writ large "Hear, O Israel, the Lord *our* God, the Lord *is!*"

A student of theology, influenced by all three, but a disciple of none, writes in summation.

God is the indefinable, indescribable, and inexpressible personality or force which makes the universe come alive.

God is infinite. Any attempt at a final definition or description of the essence of the Deity must be false, in being a delimiting of the limitless, a confining of the unconfinable. No more than any mathematical expression or measurement can approximate a description of infinity, can a verbal formulation express God. Infinity is not made recognizable by defining it as other than that which it is not. It is that plus more. So God is the uncharted plus beyond human experience and knowledge.

God operates through the heart and mind of man. But the mind cannot fully conceive nor the heart feel nor the tongue express God. We conceive but hazy notions, feel but vague echoes, and express these through the imperfect medium which is speech.

Man brings God to earth; God lifts man heavenward. The relationship of God and man is through a covenant, a mutually benefiting and mutually demanding agreement. God holds out to man the lure to holiness, the desire for the highest reaches of mind and heart. Man gives God pragmatic reality as he brings to life God's lure to holiness through patterns of relationship with fellow man.

AND FOUR POETS

In truth, it has been the poet more than the theologian who spoke to the Jew of God. Students of theology speak largely to each other. The poet opens his heart and his words find welcome in the hearts of those who share his passion. Our great poets gave expression to emotions deeply felt and passionately held by a "God-intoxicated people." Tradition teaches that "God desires the heart." What better way to know God than through the heart, and who speaks more clearly the words of the heart than the poet? The truest image of this people's concept, concern, and commitment to their Creator is found in lines of verse, rather than in theologic formulation or systems. It is no wonder then that the most basic and enduring celebration of God found in Judaism is the poetic anthology called The Psalms.

Four poets, separated in time and space, sing of God. In ancient days the Psalmist sang:

> Whither shall I go from Thy spirit?
> Whither shall I flee from Thy presence?
> If I ascend into heaven, Thou art there;
> If I make my bed in the netherworld,
>   behold, Thou art there.

> If I take the wings of the morning,
> And dwell in the uttermost part of the sea,
> Even there would Thy hand lead me,
> And Thy right hand would hold me.

In the Middle Ages, the poet-philosopher-physician, Judah Halevi, wrote:

> O Lord, where shall I find thee?
> All hidden and exalted is Thy place;
> And where shall I not find Thee?
> Full of Thy glory is the infinite space . . .

I have sought Thy nearness;
With all my heart have I called Thee;
And going out to meet Thee
I found Thee coming toward me.

In more recent times, the hassidic saint, Reb Levi Yitzhak of Berditchev, spoke to God in simple piety:

O Lord of the world, O Lord of the world!
I will sing to you a "Thou song."
Where can one find Thee,
And where can one not find Thee?
Wherever I go—Thou! and wherever I stand—Thou!
Only Thou, but Thou, always Thou, ever Thou.
If one prospers it is because of Thee, and if, God
 forbid, one has trouble, it is also Thou.
Thou art here, Thou wert here.
Thou art, Thou wert, Thou wilt be.
Thou reigned, Thou reignest, Thou wilt reign.
In heaven, Thou—on earth, Thou.
Above, Thou—below, Thou.
Wherever I turn,
Wherever I reach out—Thou!

The modern Israeli poet, Uri Zvi Greenberg, a poet who most often celebrates might, sings softly of God:

Like a woman who knows I am captive to her charms,
My God mocks me: Flee, if you only can!
And I cannot flee.

For when I flee from Him in despairing rage
And with a vow on my lips, like a sizzling coal:
"I will see him no more!"

I come back to Him again
And knock on His doors,
Like a tormented lover.

As though He had written me a love letter.

From the time the Psalmist sang to the days of Greenberg is the whole span of Western man. Empires rose and fell. Religions sprang up to contend for the hearts of men. Unknown continents were discovered, subdued, and settled. Science strode forth in giant steps. But the song of the Jewish soul remained the same:

God is. His glory fills the earth. He is before us always, everywhere. His glory fills the earth, yet "He is nigh unto those who call upon Him." The confrontation is eternal. God will always call and men will forever respond, love letter in hand.

3

WHAT IS MAN?

When a man goes on his road, a troop of angels proceed in front of him and proclaim: "Make way for the image of the Holy One, blessed be He!"

JOSHUA BEN LEVI

CREST OF CREATION

The Psalmist asks: "What is man?"

The question is as old as man himself. Answers have been given throughout the ages.

Homer:
Of all the creatures that creep and breathe on earth there is none more wretched than man.

St. Bernard of Clairvaux:
Man is nothing else than . . . a sack of dung, the food of worms.

Martin Luther:
We have altogether a confounded, corrupt and poisoned nature, both in body and in soul; throughout the whole of man is nothing that is good.

Leonardo da Vinci:
Man and the animals are merely a passage for food, a tomb for other animals, a haven for the dead, giving life by the death of others, a coffer full of corruption.

Jonathan Swift:
The most pernicious race of little odious vermin that nature ever suffered to crawl upon the surface of the earth.

The Psalmist:
What is man that thou art mindful of him?
And the son of man that thou thinkest of him?
Yet thou hast made him but little less than divine,
And hast crowned him with glory and honor.

The majestic opening verses of the Bible are the epic of creation. Upon void and chaos God caused his spirit to hover. Earth and heaven came into being at His command. Light and water and grass and trees, sun and moon and living creatures aswarm in the waters, on the earth and above the earth. The narrative moves grandly onward, upward. One senses preparation for the climax of the Lord's creative endeavor.

> And God made the beast of the earth after its kind, and the cattle after their kind, and everything that creepeth upon the ground after its kind; and God saw that it was good.

All is now in readiness for the grand finale. All of creation awaits the last culminating act of creation which gives purpose and meaning to the rest.

One can almost hear an angels' chorus in a hymn of glory, intoning:

> And God created man in His own image,
>   In the image of God created He him;
>   Male and female created He them.
> And God blessed them!
> And God said unto them:
>   Be fruitful and multiply,
>   And replenish the earth and subdue it;
>   And have dominion over the fish of the sea,
>   And over the fowl of the air, and over every
>   Living thing that creepeth upon the earth.

A question:

Why six days of labor? Why did not God create the world with one word of cosmic speech?

The answer:

When we expect a dear and cherished friend, do we not spend hours and days making ready for him? Does not one welcome labor, when one prepares an abode for his life's companion?

Man is God's chosen companion and co-worker. For him, God created a world and filled it with all that is good. More, God granted man a yet greater gift. We are taught:

> Beloved is man, for he was created in the image of God; but it was by a special love that it was made known to him that he was created in the image of God.

That man was created in the "image of God" does not mean, of course, that man bears physical resemblance to His creator.

It is to be understood in a spiritual sense. God has infused man with a spark of divinity. Each individual has something of God within himself.

Why did the rabbis consider this information so important as to call its disclosure an act of special love of God for man?

Because it teaches the supreme importance of each individual; it tells man of his *own* importance and of the equal importance of fellow man.

Fellow man's supreme importance is taught by Rabbi Akiba:

> "Thou shalt love thy neighbor as thyself" is the basic principle of the Torah. But should you say "Inasmuch as I am despised let my fellow man be despised with me; inasmuch as I am cursed let my fellow man be cursed with me." Rabbi Tanchuma taught: If you act in this manner, know who it is you despise, for "in the image of God made He him."

A question:
Why was man created first as a single individual?

The answer:
To teach that he who destroys one life in effect destroys all humanity. Had someone killed Adam, it would have been the murder of all mankind. The life of any man is no less sacred than that of Adam. Similarly, whoever saves one life, in effect saves all mankind.

The rabbis express man's infinite worth in one sentence:

One man is equal to the whole of creation.

Man is to be conscious at all times that the Holy One dwells in him, not so that he may grow in pride, but that he may be constantly aware of his responsibility to live up to his role. The teachings about man which we find in our religious literature are not to impart information but to provide instruction.

Philo states: "There is none more sacred and god-like than man"; Saadia adds that man is the purpose of creation and the axis and foundation of the world; Judah Halevi sees the seal of God in every man. These are not paeans of praise but words of challenge and admonition. They point to man's potential and urge a never ending struggle to attain it. God has made man his companion and co-worker. He has granted him the ability to soar heavenward and has shown him the direction. It is a gift that a loving father grants a beloved child. The father asks only that the son use the gift.

Rabbi Shelomo of Karlin taught:

> What is the worst thing the Evil Urge can achieve?
> To make man forget that he is the son of a king.

THE CHOOSER AND THE CHOICE

God crowned creation with man. Hardly had the crown been set up in the world than it began to tarnish. Man was disobedient and deceitful. The first generation of man murdered a brother and was all brazen innocence. Generation followed generation. Men took wives, children were born, "And the Lord saw that the wickedness of man was great in the earth." What the Lord saw then, men have experienced since. Many would agree with the gentle cynic of Jerusalem, Koheleth, the Preacher: "Man has no preeminence above the beast."

What is man, angel or beast?

Neither! says Judaism. Every man is a composite of the heavenly and the earthly. He can rise. He can fall. The choice is his.

Maimonides states:

> Man has been given free will: if he wishes to turn toward the good way and to be righteous, the power is in his own hands; if he wishes to turn toward the evil way and to be wicked, the power likewise is in his own hand.

The first Biblical teachings about man are that he can distinguish between good and evil. This knowledge makes man "as God." Man can choose to do good or evil. The power to do so was bought at a price.

The biblical narrative tells how Adam, the man, was warned by God not to eat of the tree of knowledge of good and evil or he would become subject to death. But Eve, learning that "in the day ye eat thereof, then your eyes shall be open and ye shall be as God, knowing good and evil," courted death to become "god-like," and induced Adam to do the same. And when they did "the eyes of both of them were opened." Man and woman paid dearly for "knowing good and evil." Physical pain, struggle, and death were to be their lot, not to speak of the mental anguish, the emotional upset, and the spiritual agony which this gift of the opened eyes increasingly imposes upon man. But this act of moral daring lifted man from his early role of master of the animals to companion of God.

The narrative reflects man's leap from a creature of animal-like existence to one who could contemplate his Creator, confront Him, and join Him in cosmic partnership.

A MIDRASH:

Why did not Adam and Eve eat first of the tree of life, thus assuring themselves immortality, and then eat of the tree of knowledge?

The tree of knowledge forms a hedge about the tree of life. Only he who has cleared a path for himself through the tree of knowledge can come close to the tree of life.

The knowledge of good and evil is the road to life.

Often overlooked in the story of Cain and Abel is God's challenge to the former when Cain "was very wrought":

"Why art thou wrought? and why is thy countenance fallen? If thou doest well shall it not be lifted up? and if thou doest not well, sin coucheth at the door, and unto thee is its desire, but thou mayest rule it."

It is in the power of man to do right or wrong. Temptation

is always around the corner but man, if he so desires, has the power to resist it.

It is significant that this was said to Cain before he slew Abel. Man had to be told that he had freedom of moral choice, before he could be held accountable for his acts. Knowing this, each man is held responsible for that which he does and that which he does not.

Man does not have absolute freedom of choice. He cannot determine whether he be male or female, tall or short, light or dark. But the power has been granted him to choose good or evil, the right or the wrong. "All is in the hands of heaven" said the rabbis "except the fear of heaven."

The power of choice imposes heavy responsibility. Man is to view the world as a giant balance scale. On one side is piled all the good in the world, on the other all the evil. The pointer always points to zero. His next deed, if good, will incline the pointer to good, and this world becomes a good one. If evil, his act inclines the whole world to evil. There is no greater power in the world than man's choice.

This power is a great gift which imposes a moral imperative upon man. Rabbi Nahman of Bratzlav taught:

> The world was created for the sake of the choice and the chooser. Now the master of the choice shall say: 'Only for my sake was the whole world created!'
> Therefore every man shall be watchful and strive to redeem the world and supply that wherein it is lacking at all times and in all places.

IT HATH BEEN TOLD THEE, OH MAN

Man, master of the choice, is not only given the ability to choose, but is to be told what he must choose.

> I call heaven and earth to witness against you this day, that I have set before thee life and death, the blessing and the curse; choose life, that thou mayest live, thou and thy seed.

It is man's responsibility to live, and to see to it that those who come after him will also live. There is a mystic teaching that one who causes another to lose his life is held responsible not only for the life he took, but also for the lives of potential descendants. Man lives on through his children and his children's children. To live on is to give life to countless generations. Man is duty bound to live on, because he is a sentinel placed on earth who cannot of his own accord quit his post. Man must live on because he dares not cut off from life those to whom he can give life, and their descendants "to the end of all generations."

God, having crowned creation with man, planted for him "a garden eastward, in Eden." God placed man in the garden of Eden "to work it and guard it." Man is responsible for and to the earth on which he has been placed. Its goodness is for him, but he must pay for it with labor and care. We owe this to God who created it, to ourselves and fellow man who benefit from it, and to the generations yet unborn who will inhabit it. From the beginning of time, man has been beset with responsibilities.

Rabbi Mendel of Kotsk and his disciple, Rabbi Yaakov of Radzimin, discussed the question: "To what purpose was man created?"

Said the pupil: "So that he might perfect his soul."

But the master said: "Man was created so that he might lift up the Heavens."

Wherein do master and disciple differ? To perfect the soul is to answer the demands of the Creator of the soul. To lift up the Heavens is to answer the needs of all who dwell under them.

Man's duty is to live on, as a child who lives for his Father, and as a father who lives for his children. Man is responsible to the earth which feeds him, his body which sustains him, his soul which uplifts him, and his fellow man who gives him a purpose for living.

It hath been told thee, oh man, what is good and what the Lord doth require of thee: To do justly, to love mercy, and to walk humbly with thy God.

How shall man view his world and himself in it? It is nowhere better stated than in the discourse of Rabbi Azrael in S. Ansky's play, *The Dybbuk*.

The world of God is great and holy.

In all the world the holiest land is the land of Israel. In the land of Israel the holiest city is Jerusalem; in Jerusalem the holiest place was the holy Temple, and the holiest spot in the Temple was the Holy of Holies.

In the world there are seventy nations and of them the holiest is Israel. The holiest of the people of Israel is the tribe of the Levites. The holiest of the Levites are the priests and amongst the priests, the holiest is the High Priest.

The year has three hundred and fifty-four days. Of these the holidays are the holiest. Holier than the holidays are the Sabbaths, and the holiest of the Sabbaths is the Day of Atonement, Sabbath of Sabbaths.

At a certain hour, on a certain day of the year, all these supreme holinesses met together. This took place on the Day of Atonement, at the hour when the High Priest entered the Holy of Holies and there revealed the Divine name . . .

Wherever a man stands to lift his eyes to heaven that place is a Holy of Holies. Every human being created by God in His own image and likeness is a High Priest. Each day of man's life is the Day of Atonement; and every word he speaks from his heart is the name of the Lord . . .

4

AND THOU SHALT
LOVE THE LORD,
THY GOD . . .

It is good if man can bring about that God sings within him.

ELIMELECH OF LIZHENSK

The divine sings in noble deeds.

ABRAHAM JOSHUA HESCHEL

The battle of God concealed in life is my battle.

SH. SHALOM

TO BELIEVE . . . TO LOVE

In a remarkable book about the death days of Europe's Jewry, *The Tiger Beneath the Skin*, Zvi Kolitz writes:

In the ruins of the ghetto of Warsaw, among the heaps of charred rubbish, there was found, packed tightly into a small bottle, the following testament, written during the ghetto's last hours by a Jew named Yossel Rakover.

Warsaw, April 28, 1943.

"I, Yossel, son of David Rakover of Tarnopol, a Hassid of the Rabbi of Ger and a descendant of the great, pious, and righteous families of Rakover and Meisel, inscribe these lines as the houses of the Warsaw ghetto go up in flames . . .

"I die peacefully, but not complacently; persecuted, but not enslaved; embittered but not cynical; a believer, but not a supplicant; a lover of God, but not a blind amen-sayer of His.

"I have followed Him even when He repulsed me. I have followed His commandments even when He castigated me for it; I have loved Him even when He hurled me to the earth, tortured me to death, made me an object of shame and ridicule.

"And these are my last words to You, my wrathful God; nothing will avail You in the least. You have done everything to make me lose my faith in You, but I die exactly as I have lived, crying: Eternally praised be . . . the God of vengeance, of truth and of law, Who will soon show face to the world again . . .
"Hear, O Israel, the Lord our God, the Lord is One.

"Into your hands, O Lord, I consign my soul." *

Yossel Rakover's faith was uplifted by suffering as was the faith of the Spanish exile whose cry to God introduces this

---

* Zvi Kolitz, *The Tiger Beneath the Skin*, Creative Age Press, New York, 1947.

volume. Both were echoing the steadfast, defiant faith of that classic sufferer, Job: "Yea, though He slay me, yet will I believe in Him." Such is the faith of the devout Jew when called upon to be saint and martyr.

Yet the Jew is not commanded to believe in God, for as S. D. Luzzatto wrote, "Belief cannot be commanded." We find nowhere in the Bible the command, "Thou shalt believe in the Lord thy God." The command that has become the root demand of our faith is "And thou shalt love the Lord, thy God, with all thy heart, with all thy soul, and with all thy might." It follows Israel's declaration of faith, "Hear, O Israel, the Lord our God, the Lord is One."

Belief is an emotion which is felt; love is a deed which is performed. Leo Baeck expressed it well. "In Judaism, love toward God is never a mere feeling; it belongs to the sphere of ethical activity." The admonition "to love God" introduces a paragraph which describes how the Jew begins to express his love. "And these words, which I command thee this day, shall be upon thy heart . . ." We express our love for God by knowing His will, heeding His words, fulfilling His commandments. A medieval moralist, Bahya ibn Pakuda, taught: "Our answer must be given in deeds, not words."

An answer implies a call. What is God's call to Israel? We read in Deuteronomy:

> And now Israel, what doth the Lord thy God require of thee, but to fear the Lord thy God, to walk in all His ways, and to love Him, and to serve the Lord thy God with all thy heart and with all thy soul; to keep the commandments of the Lord and His statutes which I command thee this day, for thy good.

FOR THY GOOD

A parable in the Midrash tells of a doctor who visits two patients. After examining the first, he tells the relatives that they may give him whatever he requests to eat and places no restriction upon him. But the second he restricts to a very limited diet. When asked the meaning of what he has done, he answers: "The first is about to die. There is no hope for him so I permitted him to eat whatever he desires. But the second will survive, if we take very special care of him, so for him I ordered a strict diet."

There are religions which view life here on earth only as a prelude to eternal life in the hereafter. Their purpose is to assure their adherents of eternity. Life here and now is not of crucial importance. The law which regulates earthly existence is as naught before the faith which assures life eternal. Judaism is a this-world centered religion. Its purpose is to train man to live on the earth on which God has placed him, as God desires him to live. God teaches man how to live through the law which He revealed to man, through the commandments which man is bidden to obey. Commandments, ordinances, statutes are "for thy good," to train man in the art of the good life. "The sacred commandments were given for the sake of righteousness, to arouse pious thoughts and to form character."

THE COSMIC PARTNERSHIP

God, who created the world, ordained laws of nature which give order and harmony to His universe. God, who created man, revealed to him a moral law. Man, by adhering to it, will fashion a wholesome life for himself, as Ibn Ezra taught: "The essence of all precepts is to make the heart upright"; and help in establishing order and harmony in the life of mankind, as Maimonides reminds us: "The laws concerning the relation of man to God tend to improve the moral condition of mankind." In the establishment of the moral order, a partnership must be effected between God and man. The rabbis spoke of it in the concept "Man is co-worker with the Holy One, blessed be He, in all matters of creation."

Judaism teaches a noble paradox: Whatever is by God must yet become so through man. The world is not yet finished; it is man's responsibility to enhance it. Man is not perfect but perfectible, and it is his duty to strive to attain perfection, though he knows that he must always fall short of success. In this world which is man's home, God has provided all the raw material necessary for the good life. He has instructed man how to use it and to what purpose.

Man has been granted the mind to know his duty and the heart to understand the divine charge. He has also been assured that a benevolent Divine Father stands ready to help him walk the road of life, giving him strength for the journey; to lead him back to the road if he has strayed, to lift him up if he has fallen. "In the manner man wants to walk life's road, he is helped," we are taught, "On the road man wants to travel he is led."

In turn, man is to match strength with courage, to erase error through repentance; and when he is helped up from the ground in love, he is to lift his eyes heavenward in gratitude. Above all, man is to recognize God as a Creator who is concerned and a Father who loves. Commandments are the expression of concern, and laws the product of love. As Saadia taught: "Sin is not sinful because God forbade it; God forbade it because it is sinful."

The law which God gave to man is not beyond man's knowledge or understanding, nor above man's ability to achieve and fulfil.

We read in Deuteronomy:

> This commandment is not too hard for thee, neither is it far off . . . It is not in heaven . . . neither is it beyond the sea . . . But the word is nigh unto thee, in thy mouth, and in thy heart, that thou mayest do it.

TO WALK IN ALL HIS WAYS . . .

Partnership implies mutual need. God needs man to fulfil His plan; man needs God to rise to his destiny. Co-workers must have respect for each other. How does man show his respect to God?

How does a son express his love for his father? By fulfilling to the utmost the potential which is his; by bringing into his own life the qualities which characterize the father. When these qualities are made the vehicle of fulfilment, it is the wedding of love and wisdom.

God charges His children:

Ye shall be holy, for I the Lord your God am holy."

Holiness is fulfilment for man, even as it is a quality of God. Man can achieve holiness through the imitation of God. Through his life and deeds man is to reveal the divine that has been implanted in him. Being created in the image of God is a privilege which imposes the responsibilty to be "godlike." Mortal man cannot, of course, imitate God's eternity, power, or majesty. But man can and should emulate the ethical qualities which are ascribed to God.

The Talmud teaches:

Be like God; as He is merciful and gracious, so be thou merciful and gracious. Scripture commands "Walk ye after the Lord your God." But the Lord is a consuming fire, how can men walk after Him? The meaning is by being as He is: merciful, loving, long-suffering. Mark how on the first page of the Torah God clothed the naked Adam; and how on the last he buried the dead Moses. He heals the sick, frees the captives, does good even to His enemies, and is merciful both to the living and the dead.

These qualities of concern and mercy are what bind man to God. "It is in his compassionate moments that man is nearest to God."

THE JOURNEY TOWARDS GOD

The road to God leads not away from the world, but through the world. Man can approach the Creator only through His creation. Our life on the earth on which we have been placed, with all its weal and woe, is our journey towards God. The just Creator is also the merciful Father who longs for the nearness of His children. In His love, He has given them commandments, the fulfilment of which opens gates and guides the traveler on his way.

The traveler soon finds that every act of concern and compassion, every deed of devotion and dedication, opens his eyes to new enterprises of the spirit. The rabbis express this through their teaching that "the reward for the fulfilment of a commandment is the opportunity to fulfil another."

The purpose of the journey, then, is not the destination but the journey itself. God calls man to come ever closer, not that many may reach the goal, but that all may undertake the journey. A loving father desires that his children show him love, not only because he craves their love, but primarily because they and he know that they can best express their love through the type of life he desires them to lead. The father's real craving is for such a life for his children. The prophet Jeremiah speaks the word of God: "Me, they have forsaken, and My Law, they kept not." The rabbis comment:

God says: "Let them forsake Me, so long as they keep My Law." There is an immediate pious addendum: "For through it they will return to Me."

We are taught: It is not so much that yearning for God will lead to the good life, as that the good life will bring man nearer to God.

Judaism is a law-centered religion. The Law gives direction to life; the fulfilment of the Law lifts man, the child, to the Father who beckons. We do not wait until we are overwhelmed with the desire to do right. We dare the deed, assured by the faith that the good deed will fashion noble desire, which in turn will produce the exalted deed.

REVELATION

We cannot rely on "the spirit" to move us, for we may be weighted down with spiritual lethargy or moral laziness. And, if we desire to serve God, can we permit our conscience to be our guide? It is so easy to confuse self-interest with conscience. But even if we escape this pitfall, shall we serve the Father according to our wisdom or His will? Is not the true expression of love to do that which our beloved desires rather than that which we fancy?

God is served when we place ourselves in His service. We are taught that the highest service is to respond to His command. Only when we respond to duty, to God's demand on us, do we truly serve Him. Louis D. Brandeis summed up Judaism's teaching in his challenge: "Duty must be accepted as the dominant conception in life."

The Prophet Micah preached:

It hath been told thee, O man, what is good, and what the Lord thy God requireth of thee."

The prophet's word may be read "It hath been told thee, O man, what is good, namely, what the Lord requires of thee." How does man know what the Lord requires?

The grandest scene in the Bible is of a people which but yesterday cast off its chains, coming before their God to hear His demands upon them. The opening words are: "I am the Lord, thy God, who took you out of the land of Egypt, out of the house of bondage." There follow commandments from God to man. Now, the opening statement has given rise to a variety of interpretations. Some medieval Jewish philosophers have understood it as the first and primary commandment: To believe in God. Others have viewed it as an introduction to the commandments: God has given you freedom, now you owe him obedience, favor for favor.

We would rather view all the commandments as an expression of God's love: You, children of Israel, have just experienced one manifestation of His love for you, His freeing you from slavery; now, in His love, he begins to reveal to you how you may love Him. Commandments, laws, ordinances, precepts are given you. A loving Father is beginning to teach you how to live. His word now comes to you through Moses. Later His prophets will preach to you, His sages will impart wisdom to you, the rabbis will interpret the law; and everything that the sincere disciple will disclose, to the end of time, is God's word given in love to his children.

Dr. Robert Gordis states the case for continuous revelation:

Revelation means communication; it requires *two* active participants. It depends not merely upon its infinite and divine source, but also on its finite and imperfect human instrument. Hence the idea of a progressive and growing revelation is not merely compatible with faith in its divine origin, but is the only view which reckons with the nature of the human participant in the process.

EVERY ACT MADE HOLY

God reveals His word and will, His Law. "Obedience to His Law is the noblest form of devotion to God," Moritz Lazarus wrote. The Jew can display his devotion through every aspect of his being and every act of his life. We are taught that the verse in Proverbs, "In all thy ways, know Him," means that man can serve God "even in those things which a man does for his body, by dedicating them to His service; even in food and drink, when he walks and when he sits, in lying down and in rising up and in speech. All that you do should be in service to God, or lead to His service."

Every act then, no matter how commonplace or menial, is suffused with holiness, drawing its sanctity from the purpose to which it is directed. Man does not surrender to his desires, nor does he suppress his needs. He rather sanctifies them by consecrating them to the service of God.

How well Martin Buber expresses this basic Jewish doctrine!

> One should, and one must, truly live with all, but one should live with all in holiness, one should hallow all that one does in one's natural life. No renunciation is commanded. One eats in holiness, tastes the taste of food in holiness, and the table becomes an altar. One works in holiness, and he raises up the sparks which hide themselves in all tools. One walks in holiness across the fields, and the soft songs of all herbs, which they voice to God, enter into the song of our souls . . . A husband is united with his wife in holiness, and the Shekhinah rests over them.

LET THE WICKED FORSAKE HIS WAYS

What is the difference between a wise man and a fool? The fool sometimes says wise things; even the wisest at times engages in foolishness. What is the difference between them?

Say: The fool never changes his mind. Circumstances may change, new conditions may arise, but he clings to his opinion, no matter what betides.

What is the difference between a good man and a wicked man? The wicked at times may rise to great goodness, and even the saint may fall heir to sin, as we have been taught: "There is no man that sins not." What then is the difference between them?

Say: The wicked man never changes his ways!

"The ignorant cannot be pious, nor the foolish free from sin," we are taught in *The Ethics of the Fathers*. One who does not know that man can and does sin cannot be a candidate for piety, and one who is unaware that man, having sinned, can turn away from it cannot live the good life. Just as knowledge teaches that no man is so righteous that he cannot sin, so wisdom instructs that no sinner is so corrupt that he cannot turn in repentance.

Why does man sin?

The good Father has not burdened His children with taint of sin, which was neither their desire nor their doing. "God created you upright," Saadia wrote; "it is you who soil yourselves with wickedness." The Talmud teaches that man sins, not because his is a depraved nature, but because "a spirit of foolishness has entered him."

Man the sinner is not the rebellious son who condemns his descendants with his guilt; he is rather the erring child who has foolishly gone astray. A loving Father awaits his return through repentance. We read in the Talmud:

What shall become of a sinner?

Wisdom declares: "May evil pursue the sinner."
Prophecy preaches: "The sinner shall die!"
The Law states: "Let him bring a sin offering, and he shall be forgiven."
But God promises: "Repentance shall save him."

Man is torn by conflicting desires. He wants to do right, but temptation is always beckoning. "Sin coucheth at the door, and unto thee is its desire." The rabbis saw man's nature as the arena of a continual conflict between the "good impulse" and the "evil impulse." The "evil impulse" appeals to his weakness, his lust, his greed. Religion has forged weapons with which man can withstand its onslaught. These are a wide variety of laws which train him in self-discipline and which strengthen those aspects of his personality which are allied with the "good impulse," kindness, compassion, mercy.

Man knows too that God the Father is deeply interested in His child's struggle to resist evil and do good. When man sins he turns his face away from God, but God does not turn away from man. "God's hand is stretched out to receive the repentant sinner." What does man need for repentance? Nahman of Bratzlav taught:

> Three things are requisite for repentance: seeing eyes, ears that hear, and an understanding heart.

To be moved to repentance, man must be able to judge his own conduct objectively and sincerely. His ears must be attuned to hear the teachings of sages and the lessons of experience. The heart must understand that if it has fallen, it can be lifted up. "If thou doest good, shall it not be lifted up?"

Israel Salanter reminds us that repentance is not remorse, but a serious attempt to profit from past mistakes. How does man go about repenting? He does not begin with the proclamation, "From today on I'll be a saint!" No shouting or breast-beating or heroic feats of abnegation. The repentant begins by acknowledging that he has done wrong, by resolving to change his ways, and by taking the first step toward eradication of the error. He begins by resisting the next bit of wickedness which beckons. He begins to walk the right road when he leaves the wrong road. The beginning of good is the shunning of evil. The sages taught:

> He who deliberately and forcibly restrains himself from sinning has already entered the Kingdom of Heaven.

Repentance is a joint enterprise of the cosmic co-workers, God and man. It is for man who has strayed to initiate the return. The repentant sinner is the true hero of the spirit. He has experienced sin, but now by force of his will he transcends it. Sincere penitence is the height of piety.

"Failure to repent is much worse than sin," Simha Bunam of Pshysha warned. "A man may have sinned for but a moment, but he may fail to repent of it for moments without number."

God awaits and aids the penitent, as we have been taught by Rabbi Jose:

> God says: My children, open for me the gate of repentance the width of a needle, and I will open it wide for you.

PRAYER—THE SERVICE OF THE HEART

"There is an old story, conceived by the sages and handed down from age to age, that when God had finished the world, he asked one of his angels if aught were wanting in land or sea, in air or in heaven. The angel replied that all was perfect; one thing only was lacking—speech to praise God's work. And the heavenly Father approved the angel's words, and soon thereafter he created man, gifted with the muses. This is the ancient story," wrote Philo, "and in consonance with this spirit, I say:

> "It is God's peculiar work to benefit man, and man's work to give Him thanks."

Man lifts his voice to God in moments of depression and in mood of exultation. In need, he pleads; in loneliness, he longs; beset by bewilderment, he asks for guidance. In the variety of human moods he turns for strength and uplift to his Creator. As the child shares his vexations and joys with his father, as he tells his mother his gratitude and love—so man addresses his Father in Heaven. Do mother and father demand their child's confession of gratefulness, do they ask for his expression of adoration? Does the heavenly Father need psalms of thanksgiving, garlands of gratitude?

The child, having lisped out his fear and blurted out his need, is strengthened and bolstered because a kindly, concerned parent was there to listen. What brings parents and children closer to each other than the child's whispered confidence; eyes lifted in loving gratitude; or a simple "Thank you"?

Rabbi Judah Loew wrote: "God is not dependent on being glorified by His creatures . . . But all creatures justify their creation by honoring the Lord."

Why does man pray? Answers range from "Because he is commanded" to "Because he can do naught else." The mystic tells that all of nature is engaged in prayer; the plant that turns its face to the sun, the bird soaring through the blue, the roaring lion and bleating lamb, and man gifted with voice. The legalist ordains time and form and formula of prayer. Maimonides, the rationalist, explains:

> We offer prayers to God in order to establish the principle that God observes our ways, and that success or failure do not happen by chance.

Eight centuries later, Abraham Isaac Kuk, the great rabbi with the heart of a mystic, wrote:

> Through his prayer man unites in himself all being, and lifts all creation up to the fountain head of blessing and life.

The words of the contemporary theologian, Abraham Joshua Heschel:

> Prayer is an invitation to God to intervene in our lives, to let His will prevail in our affairs; it is the opening of a window to Him in our will, an effort to make Him the Lord of our soul.

What is prayer? Is it petition to God or a sermon to ourselves? In early times it was much the former, always accompanied with pithy reminders that it should be the latter as well. In more recent times the pendulum has swung. In our classic religious literature we read of prodigious feats of prayer. But we also hear the opinion:

> We should beseech God, not to give us blessings . . . but for capacity to receive, and having received, to keep them.

Sincerity is a prerequisite for efficacious prayer. Prayer has to be ethical, and will be accepted only from him that hath clean hands and a pure heart and "hath not taken my name in vain."

"Cast down your eyes and lift up your hearts," Rabbi Jose ben Halafta advises. The prayer of the humble rises heavenward while that of the arrogant dies on cold lips. In modern times the great masters of prayer were the rabbis of the pietistic sect, the Hassidim. The Rebbe of Koretz told his disciples:

> Gold and silver become purified through fire. If you feel no sense of improvement after your prayer, you are either made of base metal or your prayer was cold.

A century ago the fashioner of neo-orthodoxy, Samson Raphael Hirsch, wrote:

> The aim of our worship is the purification, enlightenment, and uplifting of our inner selves.

In our century, an American rabbi, Julius Greenstone, taught:

> Prayer does not affect God but ourselves. In prayer the divine within us asserts itself, seeks its union with the divine in the universe, and through that becomes ennobled and glorified.

Is prayer a petition to God or a sermon to ourselves? It is both, of course! What greater sermon to ourselves than our plea to a merciful but just Father; what more effective petition before Him, than a sincere sermon to ourselves?

The Jewish service of worship contains two basic components, the *Shema* ("Hear, O Israel") and the *Eighteen Benedictions*. The former is a biblical passage commanding the worshipper always to remember God's words, and reminding him of the consequences of obedience to God's will. The latter consists of statements of praise and petition.

Judaism, though never discouraging private personal prayer, emphasizes public prayer in and with a congregation. By joining fellow worshippers in divine service, and by phrasing all petitions and confessions in the plural, the Jew demonstrates his conviction that his fate is tied to that of his fellow man. The sin of one reflects upon and is the responsibility of all. The health, well-being, and prosperity of each is cause for communal concern. Before reciting his prayers Rabbi Yehiel Michel of Zlotchov used to say:

> I bind myself to the whole body of Israel, with those greater than I, in order that they may uplift me, and with those smaller than I, in order that they may be uplifted by me.

Ten adult males (called a *minyan*) constitute the quorum needed for public worship. Where hearts unite in worship "God's presence dwells."

Rabbi Nahman of Bratzlav cautioned that an angry man is unfit for prayer, for before he can confront the Father, he must be at peace with His children. He also taught that the prayer of another in your behalf aids you more than your own prayer. He suggests that it is in man's power to be of help to fellow man in prayer as in deed. "He is a sinner," the Talmud teaches, "who refuses to pray for his fellow." We are also reminded that it would be wisdom so to live as to win for ourselves the prayers of those about us.

Intention, *kavanah,* is stressed in Judaism, as is spontaneity. Yet regular, ordered prayer is ordained, regulated in time and ordered in contents. We are ordered "Change not the form in which the sages cast the prayer." So there is a *siddur* from which prayers are read, and prescribed prayers are read morning and evening each day, and special orisons on the Sabbath and holidays.

Does not such regulation and prescription stifle the whole spirit of prayer? No, says Rabbi Joseph H. Hertz, "as if *discipline* in an army, or *laws* in a country, necessarily suppressed patriotism. In fact, rule and discipline in worship *increase* devotion: without them the noblest forms of adoration are unknown."

Rare exalted spirits can rise to the inspiration which would lead to spontaneous prayer. Man, ordinary man, cannot wait until inspiration seizes him. He should pray as he has been taught to pray, inviting prayer to fire him with inspiration.

Prayer is its own justification, but it is also a means to an end. "By prayer we lift ourselves to a world of perfection." Prayer opens our eyes to the wonder about us; it purifies our hearts, it lifts up the downcast soul; it reminds us of our responsibilities to ourselves, to our God and to our fellow man. Prayer prepares us for and urges us to righteous living. Judah Halevi admonishes:

> The influence of divine power is not seen in choice phrases and raised eyebrows, in weeping and praying and uttering empty words, not supported by charitable deeds; it is only made manifest by a pure heart and good works, which, although difficult, are performed with utmost zeal and love.

Indeed, it is argued that prayer is preparation for worship. The Union Prayer Book sums it up simply and succinctly. "We can worship Thee in holiness only as we serve our brother in love."

All we have said about God and man and the bridge of prayer can be expressed in this brief traditional prayer:

"May we all unite to do Thy will with a perfect heart."

5

LOVE THY
NEIGHBOR...

To be a man means to be a fellow man ... The respect we owe to our neighbor is not an isolated single commandment but represents rather the whole content of morality, the quintessence of our duty.

LEO BAECK

THOU SHALT LOVE

In ancient days the Jew met his God in a temple dedicated to His service on a hill in Jerusalem. Here he brought the fat of his flock and the first fruits as offerings of thanksgiving. The Levites sang psalms which spoke of God's goodness and man's gratitude. But instinctively, the folk felt that there was more to serving God than sheep, produce, and song. So the people spoke its feeling in its own language, in a legend.

Once upon a time there lived two brothers. They had neighboring farms separated by a hill. One brother was blessed with wealth, a lovely wife and many children. The other had neither wealth nor wife nor children, and he lived all alone on his small plot of ground. Now it happened one night, at harvest time, that neither brother could sleep. Each was thinking of the other.

The rich brother mused: "God has been good to me. My blessings are many. But my poor brother has nothing. How can I sleep? I'll take some sheaves from my field and leave them on his." He leaped from his bed and went to his field.

The poor brother thought to himself: "My needs are so few, with only myself to care for. But my brother has to provide for wife and children—so many mouths to feed. I'll take some of my sheaves to his field tonight." And off he went to his field.

Each brother took some sheaves from his field upon his shoulder and set out for the other's field. They met at the top of the hill, each under his burden, and each quickly understood what the other was doing. They dropped their sheaves and embraced as tears came to their eyes.

The Holy One, blessed be He, saw their act of brotherly love. He shed a tear of joy and ordained that upon this hill

His Temple should be built. For where man meets his brother in brotherly love, heaven is nearest to earth.

Twice we are bidden to love.

> *And thou shalt love the Lord thy God.*
> *Love thy neighbor as thyself.*

The two commandments are one, as the Talmud teaches: "Love God in the human beings He has created." Man expresses his love for God through the love he bears toward his fellow man. We convey our love for God not through declaration but through deed. The noblest confession of that love is through assumption of duty toward one's fellows. The pathway from man to God leads through the love of all men. "If we protect and guard His children, we show faithfulness to God," said Rabbi Akiba.

Our tradition teaches that crimes against men are sins against God, and that one who injures his fellow man commits a worse sin than one who robs the Holy Temple. A sage explained why a sin against fellow man is worse than a sin against God. "The man you harmed may have gone to an unknown place, and you will not be able to ask him forgiveness. The Lord, however, is everywhere, and you can always find Him when you seek Him."

How man can truly express his love for his Maker is best summed up by Rabbi Abraham Kuk:

To deem the worship of God the payment of tribute, under the stress of dread and terror, to some transcendent being, is to think like an idolator.

That is not what the Jew holds the worship of God to be. To him it means undying love for godly ideals, for justice, righteousness and truth.

To worship God is to embody these godly ideals and to bring about their fulfilment in the life of the nation, the individual, and the world.

To Do Justly And To Love Mercy

Let us turn then to consider these godly ideals and their fulfilment. To cherish ideals is noble, but we are bidden to add utility to nobility. The Jew is duty bound to express his ideals through deeds. A great system of law, vast in detail, even as it is exalted in purpose, has been established to enable us to bring the ideals of justice, righteousness, and truth into the arena of every day living. The Law gives sinews and muscles to beliefs and commitments. Deeds give life to ideals. To the Jew the most exalted religious expression is a good deed performed for one's fellow man.

The sage Hillel, two millennia ago, was challenged by a heathen: "Teach me all of Judaism while I stand on one foot." Hillel replied: "What is hateful to thee, do not to thy neighbor! This is the whole Torah—all of Judaism. The rest is commentary." Then he added: "Now go forth and study."

We take up the challenge to learn while "we stand on one foot" as it were, condensing in a few pages the teachings of what is the heart of our faith—the relationship of man to fellow man. We shall consider this basic concern of Judaism in the traditional Jewish mode of study: text; commentary, which carves for the text new dimensions; and law, which gives utility to both.

Micah the prophet proclaimed:

> It hath been told thee, O man,
>   What is good,
> And what the Lord doth require of thee:
> Only to do justly, and to love mercy,
>   and to walk humbly with thy God.

It Hath Been Told Thee

Man has not only been commanded to do good, but has been told what is the good he is to do, and how to do it. A righteous deed is called a *mitzvah*—a commandment. "The sacred commandments" we read in *Aristeas,* "were given for the sake of righteousness, to arouse pious thoughts and to form character." The performance of a mitzvah strengthens piety, purifies sentiments, and elevates aspirations.

What is good?

We are taught:

Submit to the yoke of heaven, excel in the fear of God and love one another.

It means:

How can one submit to the yoke of heaven? By excelling in the fear of God. How can one excel in the fear of God? By loving one's fellow man.

TO DO JUSTLY

Justice and Judaism are synonymous. The biblical command: "Justice, justice shalt thou pursue!" are words of admonition and mission. Justice is to be pursued "that thou mayest live." Justice is the ideal toward which the Jew is to strive, and the standard by which he is to direct his life.

What is justice?

Every man is equally dear in the eyes of God. Each man has equal right to benefit from the world's goods and the riches of the earth. The relationship between men is to be determined and judged, not by who they are or what they own, but by laws which apply equally to the rich and the poor, the wise and the simple, even the good and the wicked. God Himself, as it were, is subject to the laws of justice. Did not Abraham question, "Shall not the Judge of all the earth do justly?"

Why the repetition of the word justice?

Rabbi Simha Bunam explained: "Justice may be pursued only through justice. It can be established only through just means." The end does not justify the means. In truth, the means employed determine the end which is reached.

Why the word justice twice?

One refers to man and the other to God. When one acts justly towards his neighbor, it is an act of justice for God.

Another commentary suggests that the re-iteration of the word justice is designed to teach us something about litigation. A just verdict benefits both parties. The one regains that which is his; the other is kept from the sin of having that which is not his.

Only two commandments carry the injunction "to pursue" —peace and justice. "Seek peace and pursue it" and "Justice, justice shalt thou pursue." The performance of all other *mitzvot* becomes a duty only when the occasion arises. Peace and justice demand active search and pursuit. Peace is indivisible. To maintain peace here we must retain it everywhere. Justice must be pursued because it permits no neutrality. We cannot remain indifferent. When injustice is rampant, we are either the victim or the perpetrator. To remain aloof to injustice is to participate in it. There are no innocent bystanders. One who stands by while an injustice is perpetrated cannot be adjudged innocent. His failure to stand up to injustice is in violation of the commandment to pursue justice. To fulfil this mitzvah one must oppose injustice anywhere and everywhere.

Jeremiah warned:

Woe to him who builds his house by . . . injustice.

Isaiah gave challenge and instruction:

Seek justice; relieve the oppressed.

The admonition of Amos rings through the ages:

Let justice well up as waters,
And righteousness as a mighty stream.

The insistence on justice, strict justice finds expression in law.

TO LOVE MERCY

Justice having been established, mercy must be practiced.

Jerusalem was destroyed, the sages taught, because its people lived up to the strict requirements of the law of justice and did not rise above it to acts of mercy and compassion. "To do justly" is to fulfil the minimum requirement of the law. This is one's duty as a citizen. "To love mercy" is the demand of the higher law which lifts man to piety. Justice can be exacted by law or authority; mercy must flow from the heart.

Mercy is to refrain from visiting hurt upon someone else. How better to avoid hurting someone than to train oneself to know what gives pain to another and to know it so well as to actually feel it?

How is the Jew trained in the art of mercy?

We are bidden to beware of causing pain. The Talmud teaches that the Bible commands man to feel "the pain of a living creature." Thus the biblical laws:

Thou shalt not plow with an ox and an ass together.

Ibn Ezra explains:

"God hath mercy on all His creatures." The strength of the ass is not equal to the strength of the ox. It would be unmerciful to the ass to force him to try to keep up with the more powerful ox.

Thou shalt not muzzle an ox when he treadeth out the corn.

Rashi comments:

"This is the law for all animals working among food." It would be cruel to the animal to force it to go hungry in the midst of plenty.

Concern for the welfare of the animal is concretized in law.

Rabbi Judah taught in the name of Rab:

It is forbidden for a man to eat until he has fed his animals.

Indeed a man is not to buy animals until he has made provision to feed them.

Trained in mercy for animals, man can feel deeper compassion for fellow man, no matter how lowly his station. As a matter of fact, the lowlier the station, the greater must be our compassion. We are taught that God's special wards are those who have been most handicapped by fate.

On the lowest rung of the social ladder was the slave. Yet he was protected against injury by his master, for such injury would gain the slaves freedom. To take his life was a capital offense. A slave he was, but a human being as well. Samuel reminds the people that "You were permitted to have slaves for labor, not for humiliation." Maimonides admonishes: "Though the law permits us to impose hard labor on a Canaanite slave, piety and wisdom command us to be kind and just."

Slavery was early frowned upon in Israel, and it never became as significant an institution there as in Greece or in Rome.

An escaped slave had but to touch the soil of the land of Israel to gain his freedom. It was forbidden to deport him but "he shall dwell with thee, in the midst of thee, in the place which he shall choose in one of thy gates, where it liketh him best; thou shalt not wrong him."

Again and again we are admonished that special care must be taken in dealing with the weak and bereaved. To wrong a widow or an orphan, for example, is to afflict them doubly. They suffer the hurt of the wrong itself, and then again, the hurt reminds them of their unfortunate circumstance. We must become sensitive to the psychological wounds we may inflict. Such injuries are not always quite so obvious as physical hurt or monetary loss, but the anguish they cause is far greater. The Bible is profuse in its warning and the Law is alert to protect God's special words. "If thou afflict them in any wise, and they cry at all unto me, I will surely hear their cry."

Stern principles of justice are tempered with mercy as they

are translated into law. What harsher sounding statement than the *lex talionis:*

> An eye for an eye,
> A tooth for a tooth,
> A hand for a hand,
> A foot for a foot.

As a principle of justice it is a most humane pronouncement. It says that a human organ cannot be considered to have monetary value. It would be inhuman to say, for example: "an eye is valued at one hundred shekel, a foot at fifty." A human organ, serving a child of God, is above any monetary value to be stipulated. The value of an eye is an eye, of a tooth, a tooth. Justice would demand that if one gouges out the eye of his neighbor, the just recompense would be to forfeit his own eye.

This is the demand of strict justice. But to do so would not serve the cause of true justice. What it would do would be to multiply injustice by maiming another human being. To serve justice we need add mercy as we translate principle to law. The Talmudic law specifies that if one injures his neighbor, he is to make monetary restitution for the loss of limb, for the pain, for the medical costs, for the loss of income, and for the shame the injury caused. Mercy is often a necessary element in the establishment of justice.

Justice provides for capital punishment. There are a number of crimes listed in the Bible which demand the extreme penalty. In Talmudic law, however, it becomes virtually impossible to condemn any man to death. Circumstantial evidence is not accepted, nor hearsay evidence, nor even confession. The offender had to have been warned before commission of the act what his punishment would be. Two witnesses had to see the actual commission. They underwent searching examination by a collegium of judges bent on saving the life of the accused. A *sanhedrin* (court of law) which condemned one man to death in seventy years was called bloodthirsty. Rabbi Akiba and Rabbi Tarfon said, "If we had been in the *sanhedrin* none would ever have been put to death."

The sanctity of human life invites mercy to temper the machinery of justice. True fulfilment of justice requires mercy. The Zohar taught:

There is no true justice unless mercy is part of it.

Mercy is to be extended even to the wicked. A story illustrates.

A respected woman once came to ask advice from the rabbi of Apt. The instant he set eyes on her he shouted: "Adulteress! You sinned only a short while ago, and yet now you have the insolence to step into this pure home!"

From the depths of her heart the woman replied: "The Lord of the world has patience with the wicked. He is in no hurry to make them pay their debts, and He does not disclose their secret to any creature, lest they be ashamed to turn to Him. Nor does He hide His face from them. But the rabbi of Apt sits there in his chair and cannot resist revealing at once what the Creator has covered."

From that time on, the rabbi of Apt used to say: "No one ever got the better of me except once—and then it was a woman."

TO WALK HUMBLY WITH THY GOD

Many and great were the accomplishments of Moses. He molded tribes of slaves into a "kingdom of priests and a holy nation." He brought man to God and introduced God to man. He created Israel. Yet what phrase is chosen to describe him, what quality is admired above all others? "And the man Moses was very humble."

Humility is the quality that ennobles all others. We are taught:

Just as a house is incomplete without the humble doorstep, so is a person, regardless of all other virtues, incomplete without humility.

It makes us see that which we are and that which we have in truer and healthier perspective. Abilities are gifts to be shared freely. Prosperity does not justify pride, but prods us to responsibility. It constantly reminds us of our dependence on God and on our fellow man.

Said Rab Hisda:

Concerning a man who is arrogant, the Holy One, blessed be He, says: "I and he cannot dwell together in this world."

Arrogance is a denial of God, certainly a rejection of God as man's Protector and Helper.

The humble man "causes the Divine Presence to dwell with man on earth." For humility acknowledges God's dynamic presence in the affairs of man and invites his concern and guidance. Man's dependence on his fellows is movingly expressed by Ben Zoma:

Blessed be He who created all these people to attend to my needs. How much Adam had to toil! He had to plow and plant, cut and bind sheaves, thresh and winnow grain, grind and sift flour, and knead and bake before he could cut a piece of bread. He had to shear and wash wool, hatchel and dye and spin and weave and sew before he had a shirt to put on. But I rise in the morning and find everything ready for me.

Desiring humility, how shall a man conduct himself? The Baal Shem taught through a story:

Once upon a time there lived a king, who heard that a humble man is granted long life. So he put on old garments, left his palace for a small hut, and ordered all to treat him as a peasant and not as a king. But when the king examined himself, he found that he was prouder than before, proud of his seeming humility. A philosopher told him: "Live like a king; dress like a king; let people honor you as king; but be humble in your inmost heart."

AND WALK HUMBLY WITH THY GOD

The prophet's words ask not only humility but that man walk with God. "Noah was, in his generations, a man righteous and whole-hearted. Noah walked with God." The righteous man walks with God.

How "to walk with God" is spelled out in the nineteenth chapter of Leviticus, in the section called *The Holiness Code.*

"Ye shall be holy" the challenge issues, "for I the Lord your God am holy."

There follows a series of commands, ethical and ritual, which lead man to holiness and which are the expression of his holiness. "Holiness," Rabbi Joseph H. Hertz wrote, "is not so much an abstract or a mystic idea, as a regulative principle in the everyday lives of men and women."

We turn now to some of the "regulative principles" in this Code of Holiness.

FOR THE POOR AND THE STRANGER

Text:
Thou shalt leave them for the poor and for the stranger.
If thy brother be waxen poor . . . thou shalt uphold him.

Commentary:
Charitable endeavor is as old as the Jewish people. The Bible makes provision for systematic aid for those in need. From Biblical times on, the Jew has always considered it a prime religious duty to share what he has with those in need. We have used the phrase "religious duty to share" rather than the word "charity." The word does not adequately convey the Jewish concept of responsibility for the proper sharing of God's bounties.

Charity is subjective, depending on the giver's good will.

The Hebrew word for charitable endeavor is *tzedakah*. It is usually translated by the word charity, but its literal meaning is righteousness, justice. Judaism conceives of helping those in need not merely as an act of helpfulness motivated by sympathy or compassion, but rather as the religious duty to erase injustice and establish righteousness. Our faith teaches that if a man does not have enough to eat, or if a family does not have proper clothing or shelter or security, it is a condition of injustice for it upsets the equilibrium of the moral world.

The person who aids in doing away with this condition thus erases injustice and establishes justice. He thereby fulfils the Biblical injunction, "Justice, justice shalt thou pursue." In Judaism, it is the duty of man to establish and sustain justice. Thus it is the duty of man to do away with the injustice of poverty.

Judaism teaches that all wealth belongs to God. The Psalmist proclaimed, "The earth is the Lord's and the fullness thereof." The rabbis remind us: "If thou hast given charity, thou hast not given of thy own, but of His"; and they say that God, as it were, reminds man:

Thou art my steward. If I have given thee ought, thou owest it to me. Hence give me of my own.

God is the Father of all, and all men are therefore brothers. All the wealth of the world belongs to the Father. All should have a just share of it, as brothers would share the inheritance of their father. It is significant that when the Bible speaks to us about our less fortunate fellow man, it reminds us that he is our brother. In most cases when the Bible speaks of a poor man the term "brother" is used. For example:

If thy brother be waxen poor, and sell his possessions . . .
nor shut thy hand from thy needy brother
Thou shalt surely open thy hand unto thy poor and needy brother.

The purpose of this constant reminder that the poor man is "thy brother" was to keep us continually aware that brotherly and loving treatment is due to all, but particularly to a poor man who needs it most.

A gentle reception, a kind word of encouragement, are often more important than alms. "He who gives a coin to a poor man," say the Sages, "is blessed with six blessings, but he who encourages him with kind words is blessed with eleven blessings."

The poor man must not be embarrassed by the manner in which charity is given. "Secret giving" is ordained by the rabbis. Jewish law demands that the poor be respected and accorded every privilege and honor due to any man. Judaism further speaks of the poor as God's wards. His special concern is for them, very much as a father shows special consideration and warmth toward an unfortunately handicapped child. We are to look upon the poor as men of honesty and integrity who have come upon evil ways. It is our duty to care for them and set them upon their own feet again.

Though Judaism respected the person of the poor, it did not glorify poverty. Poverty was considered among the worst of afflictions. Among all the sufferings, say the rabbis, none is harder to bear. The greatest hardship connected with poverty is the loss of independence, the lowering of the dignity of the individual. It was therefore considered a degenerating force. It is harmful to the individual caught up in its coils, for it diminishes his dignity. It is bad for the community, for injustice is in its midst in which lie the seeds of strife and contention.

But the poor are here. What can be done to guard against violating the dignity of the poor? What can be done to preserve their self-respect? Biblical law had a wonderful answer. In an agricultural society man lived from the fruit of the land he tilled. Wealth was the produce the land provided. There were poor people during Biblical times who needed help. The simplest and most efficient way to give a poor man help would have been for the farmer to gather his harvest, bring it to his storehouse, and then have the poor line up at the door and each receive his dole. To this Judaism said *No!* This may be an efficient system, but it is a heartless one. Judaism sacrificed efficiency for humaneness. It refused to compel one human being to stretch out a beggar's hand to a fellow man. This should not be done to a child of God. But still the poor man needed food. What was done? The law reads:

> And when ye reap the harvest of your land, thou shalt not wholly reap the corner of thy field, neither shalt thou gather the gleaning of thy harvest. And thou shalt not glean thy vineyard, neither shalt thou gather the fallen fruit of thy vineyard; thou shalt leave them for the poor and for the stranger.

The corner of the field, the fallen fruit, and the gleanings could not be touched; they belonged to the poor and to the stranger. To the owner of the field, this law said: "You have a field, you worked it, you grew a crop, so it is yours. But you have a partner in your enterprise. Your partner is God. He gave the field fertility. He caused the sun to shine and the rain to fall and the fruit to ripen. Part of the harvest is His. His share is the corners, the gleanings, and the fallings. He is a good and merciful Father. Who would a father want to have his share? Why, those of his children who need it most—the poor and the stranger. Leave part of the harvest on the field, for it is theirs."

To the poor and the stranger, the law said: "You are poor and hungry, but you have a merciful Father. He wants you to have His share of the harvest, for you need it. Go on the field and gather up your harvest." After the owner of the field left, the poor and the stranger went out to gather *their* harvest. Not alms or dole, but *their* own. The work of harvesting gave them new worth in their own eyes, worth and dignity as they toiled to gather in their crop. They were poor, but they were human beings, children of a Father who was good and who cared.

Perhaps the finest statement on this subject in the Jewish tradition is the eight degrees of charity listed by Maimonides. They are listed in ascending order of merit.

1. He who gives grudgingly.
2. He who gives cheerfully but not enough.
3. He who gives a sufficient sum but is asked.
4. He who gives before being asked, but directly to the poor man.
5. The poor man knows from whom he takes, but the giver knows not the recipient.
6. The giver knows to whom he gives, but the recipient knows not the giver.
7. The giver knows *not* to whom he gives, nor does the recipient know from whom he receives.
8. The *highest* form: To strengthen the hand of the poor by giving him a loan, or to join him in partnership, or to find him work. In brief, to help him out of his poverty, to help him establish himself.

The Law:

It is a positive commandment to give charity to the poor. As it is written, "Thou shalt open thy hand to him . . . that thy brother may live with thee."

Everyone is bound to give charity to the poor according to his ability. Even if he can give little, he should not refrain, for his little is as precious to the Holy One as the bounty of the rich.

How much shall be given to a poor man? Enough to supply his needs. How much should a person give to the poor? The first year, one tenth of his capital; thereafter, one tenth of his income. This is the ordinary way. The better way is to give one fifth.

As to the one who persuades another to give, his merit is greater than that of the giver. He who gives grudgingly, with a downcast countenance, even if he gave a thousand gold pieces, he has lost the merit and reward.

It is forbidden to turn away a poor man who asks for charity.

It is more meritorious to give a loan to a poor man than to give him charity.

Dr. Solomon Schechter sums it all up.

According to Israel's law no man has a right to more than bread, water and wood, as long as the poor are not provided with the necessaries of life.

And in Practice:

The words of Maimonides are both description and admonition:

We have never seen or heard of a Jewish community without some communal charity fund.

In Talmudic times, the collection and disbursement of charity was carried on by the most distinguished leaders of the community. Each community had a fund for support of the indigent. In medieval days, the responsibilities cast upon the communities became all the greater, for persecutions produced a class of itinerant poor, who had to be supported as they sought refuge, and prisoners and captives, who had to be ransomed. There developed such institutions as the communal inn; the *kuppah,* or general charity coffer; *tamchoi,* immediate day to day relief; and tithe pacts entered into by families.

The family of Rabbi Asher b. Yehiel agreed in 1346:

We, the undersigned, accept an ordinance which we have in the handwriting of our father, Rabbi Asher, and which he worded thus:
"Hear my son the instruction of thy father, and do not forget the law of thy mother." Seeing that in the land whence we are come hither to Spain, our fathers and fathers' fathers were wont to set aside for charitable purposes a tithe of all their business profits, in accordance with our sages' proscription, we hereby undertake to follow in their footsteps, and have received upon ourselves the obligation to devote to the poor one-tenth of our profits earned in business, derived from loan of capital or from commercial undertakings. Three-fourths of this tithe we hand over to a kuppah, which shall be administered by two treasurers. This duty we undertake for ourselves and for our children.

In every European Jewish community, each Jew felt obligated to be a member of one or more charitable societies.

Among these were organizations whose purpose was to provide for the needy: clothing; education for children; dowries and trousseaus; burial costs; medical needs; legal expenses; nurses for orphaned children; food for prisoners; ransom for captives.

Moritz Lazarus reports in his *Jewish Ethics:*

> The Berlin Jewish community supported a society for the aid of mourners for one hundred and fifty years. Its object was to furnish assistance to poor families exposed to want through the death of a member, in view of the fact that the religious law enjoined the cessation of work during the days of mourning. Out of deference to the sensibilities of the recipients, the following arrangements were made: Two locked boxes were sent to every house of mourning, alike of the rich and the poor. Box No. 1 contained a sum intended for the needy. It was accompanied by its key in a sealed package and by a letter requesting the recipient to open the box and empty it. In proportion to his needs he might retain the whole or part of its contents. If he required no assistance, he was requested to put the whole sum in Box No. 2. Besides, the well-to-do were requested to add to the contents of Box No. 2 a contribution over and above the amount transferred to it from Box No. 1. Compliance with this request enabled the association to accomplish its object. Box No. 2 remained unopened for some time during its passage from family to family, so that no one, not even the directors of the society, could be aware of the identity of the givers and takers.

The noble tradition of exemplary fulfilment of the "religious duty to share" has continued to the present day. There is not a Jewish community without an active welfare fund to meet local, national, and overseas needs. The Jewish community of America has set high standards of concern and generosity which have won the admiration of others. The social welfare institutions and techniques developed, homes for the aged and the orphaned, settlement houses, united charity funds, have been widely emulated.

TO FELLOWMAN

Text:

Ye shall not steal; neither shall ye deal falsely, nor lie one to another.

Commentary:

The Rabbis taught:

There are seven classes of thieves. The first among them all is he who steals the mind of his fellow creatures.

The mind of another is "stolen" through misinformation, misrepresentation, and flattery. This is an offense to human dignity. More serious still is to steal the good opinions which others may have of someone. If we steal a man's property we diminish his wealth. To steal his good name is to diminish his personality. Human rights are more sacred than property rights. A violation against them is a greater crime against man and sin before God.

The Law:

It is forbidden to steal the mind of any person, i.e. to fool him through words, even though he suffers no monetary loss thereby.

A man may not invite another to dine when he knows that the invitation will be refused. One may not offer a present to another if he knows it will not be accepted. There is in this the element of "stealing the mind."

Commentary:

The Hebrew word for truth is *emet*. It is composed of the first, middle, and last letters of the Hebrew alphabet. So truth must be at the beginning and at the end and everywhere between. Truth is the seal of God. The Rabbis warn that God hates those who say one thing with the mouth but have another in their hearts, and remind us that the penalty of a liar is that he is not believed when he speaks the truth.

"Truthfulness must be moral," wrote Dr. Hertz; "it ceases to be truthfulness and becomes an abominable form of lying when it is used as a tool of revenge or malice in order to ruin another or for putting him to open shame."

Text:

Ye shall not swear by my name falsely, so that thou profane the name of thy God, I am the Lord.

Commentary:

If thou hast stolen, thou wilt end by falsely denying, lying and swearing by My name to a falsehood.

Text:

Thou shalt not go up and down as a talebearer among thy people.

Commentary:

The pen is mightier than the sword, but mightier still is the tongue. Life and death are in the power of the tongue. Its tremendous power is told in a pithy anecdote.

Rabbi Simeon had a servant, Tabbai. The rabbi asked his servant to go out and buy him something good. Tabbai returned from the market with a tongue. "Now," said Rabbi Simeon, "buy me something bad." The servant returned from his errand. In his hand was a tongue. Tabbai explained: "The tongue is the source of good and evil. When it offers something good, what can be better? But when it speaks something bad, what can be worse?"

He who slanders his fellow man, a rabbi taught, is as though he kills him. To deprive someone of his good name and the respect due him is to take from him that which makes life worth living. Another sage adds that to slander a fellow man is to deny God in Whose image he was created. To malign a human creature is to defy his creator.

There is a vast literature in Judaism about the sin of "the evil tongue"—gossip, tale-bearing, slander. It is considered as sinful as the cardinal sins: idolatry, immorality, and bloodshed.

The rabbis point out that "the evil tongue" is not to speak a lie, but to tell the truth. It is the truth spoken maliciously to hurt one's fellow. Aaron and Miriam were punished for speaking about Moses. They spoke the truth, but it was a truth calculated to cause pain to their brother.

Slander is compared to an arrow. An arrow kills from afar; slander spoken in one place can deprive a person of his reputation and even his life in a far distant place. When Rome was mistress of the world and had a pro-consul in Syria who ruled the Near East, there was a saying in Palestine, "What is spoken in Syria can kill in Rome; what is spoken in Rome can kill in Syria."

"Why is the tongue compared to an arrow? If a man draws a sword to kill his fellow man, the latter will plead with him for mercy and the man will repent and replace the sword in the scabbard. But an arrow, once it is loosed from the bow, can never be brought back." So it is with the tongue. What it has once spoken cannot be withdrawn or controlled.

Man must not only refrain from speaking ill; he must also take care not to create an opportunity for others to do so. Maimonides states that it is forbidden to praise a man to his enemies, for praise will only motivate his enemies to speak against him.

Just as it is wrong to speak ill, so it is sinful to listen. "Slander kills three," the Talmud says. "He who speaks it, he who listens, and the one about whom it is spoken. And the listener is more guilty than the teller. If there were no listeners, there would be no tellers." There would not be so many open mouths if there were not so many attentive ears.

The most dangerous thing about gossip and tale-bearing is that the temptation is so great. It does not seem like an overt act of wrongdoing. The evil results are not immediately seen. The crime cannot always be pinned on the guilty. The tools are always at hand, and the victim does not have to be present.

In a thousand different ways Judaism warned against the crime and sin of "the evil tongue." Thrice daily the Jew offers this special personal prayer to God and admonition to himself:

O Lord, guard my tongue from evil and my lips from speaking guile.

The Law:

What is "tale-bearing"? One who goes from person to person speaking about another: "Thus said so and so," "This is what I heard about him." Even if he speaks the truth and there is no harm in his words, this is the "tale-bearing" forbidden by the law.

A greater sin than this is "the evil tongue," to speak derogatorily of fellow man, even if it be the truth.

How far does "the evil tongue" apply? One asks another, "Where can I find fire?" He replies, "In the house of so and so, for he has much meat and fish and they are always cooking there." This is "the evil tongue."

There are things which are near "the evil tongue" (and sinful). For example: "Stay away from so and so. I don't want to tell you what happened to him or what he did."

Text:

Neither shalt thou stand idly by the blood of thy neighbor.

Law and Commentary:

A biblical law: The body of a slain man is found in a field and no one knows who killed him. First it is determined which city is nearest the scene of the crime. Then the elders of that city take a heifer, bring it to a flowing stream, break its neck, wash their hands and say:

"Forgive, Oh Lord, Thy people Israel, whom thou hast redeemed, and suffer not innocent blood to remain in the midst of Thy people." "And," the Bible states, "the blood shall be forgiven them."

From this we learn that the populace of the town in which or near which a crime was committed shared the guilt and were stained by the crime. Forgiveness had to be asked because when there is evil abroad everyone is involved.

Before the elders could ask forgiveness, the leaders of the community had to take the oath:

"Our hands have not shed this blood nor have our eyes seen it."

The sages, in comment on this strange law, ask: "Could it occur to anyone that the elders and the judges were the murderers? Why then should they take such an oath?"

Their answer: The force of their oath is this: "It did not happen that he came to us hungry and we did not feed him; or that he came to us a stranger and we expelled him from town."

Only when the leaders of the community could truthfully say: "We fed him when he was hungry, we befriended him when he was friendless," could they truly add, "Our hands have not shed this blood; neither have our eyes seen it."

Text:

Thou shalt not hate thy brother in thy heart.

Commentary:

The builders of the Tower of Babel contended against God, but because they loved their fellow men, they were merely scattered. The men of Sodom and Gomorah had hatred in their hearts for their fellow men and God blotted them out from this world and the next.

Text:

Thou shalt love thy neighbor as thyself.

Commentary:

What does it mean to love our neighbor as we love ourselves?

The Baal Shem explained:

How does one love himself? A person does not look for reasons to love himself. Man does not say: "I am nice, I am smart, I am generous, therefore I am deserving of my love." No. We love ourselves knowing our weaknesses, our shortcomings, our meanness, our vices. In the same manner we are to love our fellow men. To love for a reason is to love the reason, not the person. The reason departs, the love with it. True love is love without a reason.

Love thy neighbor as thyself.

It is easy to have kindly feeling toward those below us economically, socially, intellectually. This is not love; this is pity. Love your neighbor when he is *like* you, your equal, your competitor in wealth, in status, in intellect.

I am bidden to love my neighbor. If he is not my neighbor should I not love him? Am I not obligated to love everyone, everywhere? In truth, it is far easier to love someone, somewhere than to love my neighbor. If I train myself to love my neighbor whose life touches mine, impinges on mine, crowds mine, I will be able to love everyone everywhere.

The true answer is found some verses later.

Text:

And if a stranger sojourn with thee in your land . . . thou shalt love him as thyself.

Commentary:

Hermann Cohen observed:

The alien was to be protected, although he was not a member of one's family, clan, religious community, or people; simply because he was a human being. In the alien therefore man discovered the idea of humanity.

Rabbi Israel Salanter loved the sunshine because it shone equally on all without discrimination.

Rabbi Moshe Leib of Sasov taught us how to love our fellow man. Said he: A peasant taught me what is true love of fellow man. He was sitting in an inn drinking with a companion. Suddenly he turned to him and asked:

"Do you love me?"

"I love you very much."

"If you love me, tell me what gives me pain?"

"How would I know that?"

"If you don't know what gives me pain, how can you say you love me?"

To love one's fellow man, Rabbi Moshe taught, is to know what gives him pain and to bear the burden of his sorrow.

It is told of Rabbi Moshe Leib that whenever he saw anyone else's suffering, either of spirit or body, he shared it so earnestly that the other's suffering became his own. Once someone expressed his astonishment at his capacity to share in another's troubles.

"What do you mean, share?" said the rabbi. "It is *my own* sorrow; how can I help suffer it?"

To Rabbi Moshe Leib someone else's pain was his own.

When do I truly love my neighbor? When his pain is my sorrow.

Rabbi Moshe was expounding to his disciples.

"There is no quality and no power of man that was created to no purpose. Even base and corrupt qualities can be uplifted to serve God."

A bystander challenged him:

"You say even base, corrupt qualities can be used to serve God. Very well, how can the denial of God be used to serve Him?"

"Even that," Rabbi Moshe Leib replied. "If someone comes to you and asks your help, you should not turn him away with pious words, saying, 'Have faith! Take your troubles to God.

He will help you.' No! You should act as if there were no God, as if there were only one person in all the world who could help this man—you!"

YOU!

6

THE PEOPLE OF THE BOOK

And thou shalt teach them to thy children.

DEUTERONOMY

Every Jew, rich or poor, or even a beggar; healthy or not, young or old, is obliged to study Torah.

MAIMONIDES

The people of Neshwies . . . wore rags on their feet and ate white bread only on the Sabbath, but no child went without schooling.

MORRIS RAPHAEL COHEN

THOU SHALT STUDY . . .

It was Mohammed who called the Jews "The People of the Book." "The Book" represents to the Jew a way of life rooted in justice and directed by the laws of morality. But "The Book" is more than a symbol. Ours is a Scripture-centered faith. H. G. Wells did well to call Judaism a "literature-sustained religion."

The law of right and the rule of might are forever contending for the allegiance of man.

Rabbi Eleazar taught:

> The Book and the Sword came down from Heaven wrapped together. Said the Holy One, blessed be He: "If you will keep what is written in the Book, you will be safe from the rule of the Sword. If not, you are delivered to it."

Religious literature contains the laws of righteous living which assure well-being and establish peace. It is a Jew's first duty to learn the principles, laws, and ordinances of his faith. The pursuit of this knowledge is a life-long task. Without it he courts communal strife and personal tragedy. Possessed of this knowledge, the Jew can live a disciplined and dedicated life which is the basis of a peaceful and happy society. Maimonides called the advancement of learning "the highest commandment."

Judaism maintains that virtue can be taught and that a person can be trained to goodness. Goodness begins with knowledge and understanding. "The ignorant do not fear sin," we read in the *Ethics of the Fathers,* "nor can the unlearned be pious."

A few words are in order on the method of religious instruction in Judaism. Moses, founder of the faith and fashioner of the people, is not called prophet, seer, or saviour, but "Moses our Teacher." The prophet preaches, the seer inspires, the saviour promises salvation, the teacher instructs. The Hebrew word which is used to encompass all our religious literature is *Torah,* which literally means "teaching." The good teacher does not inculcate by rote. Indeed, Judaism has no need for memorized catechisms. The teacher of the ways and laws of life instructs his pupil by having him relive the experience of others; by engaging him in conversation; by challenging him to arrive at his own conclusion. The decision is then not thrust upon the student so that he accepts in fear or rejects in rebellion; it is the student's own, arrived at out of vicarious experience, serious consideration, and widened wisdom.

Jewish religious literature, be it historic incident, ethical admonition, or statement of law, invites comment and discussion. Professor Edmond Cahn, a student of legal systems, points out that while all other systems of law record the conclusions, the Talmud alone contains the "give and take" which leads up to the conclusion or decision. The question remains moot, thus inviting continuing comment and discussion—which indeed is still engaged in today. The book makes the student the contemporary of the sages of all ages. Through study of the text, he engages them in conversation. He enters into a disputation which began in ancient Palestine, continued in Babylonia, was commented upon in medieval France, and was reopened in eastern Europe two centuries ago. The ongoing discussion is recorded in commentaries, and further commentaries upon these in turn, which stimulate renewed consideration and invite the eager student to enter the fray.

Conversation, discussion, argumentation can take place only where the issue is unresolved, where premises abound but conclusions are left open. The Jewish student-scholar approaches a religious text with all reverence. Nahmanides wrote:

> My desire and delight is to follow the early authorities. But I do not consider myself "a donkey carrying books." I will explain their methods and I revere their worth, but . . . I will plead, in all modesty, my right to judge with mine own eyes . . . The Lord gives wisdom in all times and in all ages.

Truth asks a touch of questioning and just a strain of skepticism. This is the necessary ingredient for true scholarship, and Judaism encourages it. A modern Israeli writer has caught this spirit. Writes Hayyim Hazaz:

> That's also a Jewish characteristic, very, very Jewish: to believe with absolute faith, with glowing faith, with all their hearts and souls, and all the same just very slightly not to believe, the tiniest little bit, and that tiny little bit is the decisive thing.

Solomon Schechter, himself a scholar of ancient texts, stated: "It is not by a perpetual Amen to every utterance of a great authority that truth or literature gains anything."

This method challenged creative minds, for it encouraged the fullest exercise of the intellectual faculties. The ancient words could not only be studied, discussed, and argued, but also expanded, refined, and applied. Study became the highest religious pursuit, for how could one serve God better than to know His word and to give it currency and application in one's own life? "The beginning of wisdom is the reverence of the Lord." The attainment of wisdom—knowledge and understanding—leads in turn to the truer reverence of God.

The Mishnah teaches:

> These are the things, of which a man enjoys the dividends in this world, while the principal remains for him for the world to come; they are: honoring father and mother, deeds of loving kindness, regular attendance at the house of study and prayer, morning and evening, hospitality to wayfarers, visiting the sick, dowering the bride, attending the dead to the grave, devotion in prayer, and making peace between man and his fellow; but the study of the Torah is equal to them all, for it leads to them all.

THE STUDY OF TORAH

What is Torah?

A Torah is a parchment scroll of the Pentateuch which is read in the synagogue on the Sabbath, holidays, Monday, and Thursday.

The Torah refers to the Pentateuch or Five Books of Moses itself.

Torah, in the words of Louis Ginzberg, "is an expression for the aggregate of Jewish teachings."

The study of Torah is considered the noblest pursuit of man. Education was esteemed above all other pursuits, and the *talmid haham* (scholar) was the ornament of a community. The Bible makes the education of the young a religious duty. For almost two thousand years, universal elementary education for boys has been a Jewish communal responsibility. The Talmud records:

> Joshua b. Gamala instituted that teachers should be appointed in every province and in every city, and children about the age of six or seven placed in their charge.

A medieval Jewish authority, Israel Al-Nakawa, wrote:

> The education of the young is a communal obligation. Every community must provide teachers for the children. A city without pupils is doomed.

Today each congregation has a religious school for its children, and most allocate the major portion of the synagogue budget for the school. So preeminent was study in the Jewish scale of values that Judah the Prince stated:

> The studies of school children may not be interrupted even for the building of the holy Temple.

Nor was this sentiment limited to leaders and scholars. How better to know the soul of a people than through its lullabies? What did Jewish mothers sing to their sons?

What is the best career?
My son will study Torah!

Why study?

To fulfil one's obligations to God and fellow man.

"The purpose of the laws of the Torah," Maimonides taught, "is to promote compassion, loving kindness, and peace in the world."

To perfect oneself.

Rabbi Israel Salanter reports:

Before studying ethics I blamed the whole world and justified myself; after I started the study, I blamed myself and also the world; but finally I blame only myself.

For its own sake.

Elijah, Gaon of Vilna, is quoted saying:

Were an angel to reveal to me all the mysteries of the Torah, it would please me little, for study is more important than knowledge.

Study was not merely preparation for life. It was life itself, and so continued on through life. In European communities, almost every man was a member of a study group, and many devoted hours daily to the pursuit of knowledge. Young and old alike were caught up in the zealous and exemplary fulfilment of the commandment to study diligently.

THE BOOK OF BOOKS

The book of books is the Bible. In Hebrew it is called *TaNaKh*, the abbreviation for its three subdivisions *Torah* (Pentateuch), *Nevi-im* (Prophets), and *Kethubim* (Writings).

The Bible is not a book but a library of books. It consists of:

Historical portions telling of the birth and growth of the Jewish people, slavery in Egypt and emancipation, a Promised Land and the journey toward it, tribes who were forged into a nation, kings who ruled and prophets who admonished, faithfulness to God and godly ideals, and corruption of faith and folk, destruction and exile, and return, ancient memories and new and exalted destiny.

Laws, which disciplined lives, bound base instincts, and developed noble aspirations and compassionate conduct; which fashioned a slave people into a "kingdom of priests and a holy nation."

Writings of poets, who spoke the variety of human moods in the Psalms and celebrated the love of man for maid in the "Song of Songs."

Wisdom teachers who gave sage advice in "Proverbs."

The Book of Job which asks today as then, "why do the righteous suffer?"

Koheleth, the sage of Jerusalem, looking for meaning in this enterprise we call life.

The Bible is as wide as life itself, as deep as sorrow, as elevating as happiness. It reveals and hides. It teaches humility, yet tells man of his potentialities and urges their realization. Its influence on western civilization is summed up by Israel Zangwill:

From century to century, even to this day, throughout the fairest regions of civilization, the Bible dominates existence. Its vision of life moulds states and societies. Its Psalms are more popular in every country than the poems of the nation's own poets. Beside this one book with its infinite editions . . . all other literature seems "trifles light as air."

Yet, for all its popularity, the Bible is a difficult book. It is a work not to be skimmed or even read, but studied. Traditionally, a Jew always studied the Bible with one or more commentaries. In the most popular editions of the Hebrew

Bible, the text is an island in a sea of commentaries. A Jewish scholar of the last century, Nahman Krochmal, states:

> Reading the Bible will in itself not satisfy the needs of our faith; there must go with it proper interpretation and necessary understanding.

The first step toward "understanding" is to consider the question "What is the Bible?" No single answer has sufficed. Through the centuries, most have considered it the revealed word of God to Moses at Sinai, and through inspired prophets in later generations. Others see the Bible as the record of the spiritual adventure of a people seeking God and learning to serve Him through striving for ethical perfection. A Talmudic sage warns that "A Biblical verse cannot be deprived of its literal meaning," while a medieval scholar, Abba Mari, asserts "From Creation to Revelation all is parable." To Franz Rosenzweig, a modern scholar, "The Bible is a parable of man's advance to the family, to the tribe, to a nation with a national ideal, to a nation with a universal ideal."

Who is right? Tradition has given the answer to all differences and disputations "for the sake of heaven"—both are the words of the living God." The Baal Shem taught: "The Torah is eternal, but its explanation is to be made by the spiritual leaders of Judaism . . . in accordance with the age." Each generation, each diligent student knows the Bible in accordance with his ability, understands it in response to his needs, and is influenced by it to the degree of his commitment to the faith which it teaches.

The uncompromising fundamentalist accepts literally every word as written. He neither permits nor feels the need for interpretation. The rationalist traditionalist accepts the words as they are, but subjects them to "rational" interpretation. Thus to him the days of creation, for example, are not days as we know them but "days in the eyes of God"—long eras of time. He accepts the Bible as literal truth, but attempts, where he feels it necessary, to give it interpretation which would sound rational. The modernist accepts that which is in consonance with his reason or experience, or the reason and experience of the best minds of his day.

Are the opening chapters of Genesis scientific fact and historic truth or are they myth? To the fundamentalist they are fact and truth. The modernist calls them myth. But there is a growing body of opinion which says they are neither and both; they are "true-myths."

It is argued that the Bible is not a book of science nor even a book of history. It is a book of religion, teaching man about God and himself, his relationship to God, to the cosmos, to himself, and to fellow man. It is a religious tract exhorting him, in manner direct and subtle, to choose the good life; and it instructs him how he may do so. It abounds in religious truths. These truths often find expression through myths. A "true-myth" is a religious truth or insight expressed through a legend, a parable, or a fable. The Bible is to be viewed through "the category of significance." Indeed, Maimonides wrote in his *Guide To The Perplexed:*

> Every narrative in the Torah serves a certain purpose. It helps to establish a principle of faith or to prevent wrong or injustice among men.

The question to be asked about an event or incident is not: "Is this literally true?" but "What is its significance? What religious teaching does it convey?" Thus, in the category of significance, it is unimportant whether the world was created in six days, six years, or six million years. The religious truth couched in myth form is that the world was created by a supreme intelligence. There is therefore order and meaning in the world. It is not a haphazard coming together of atoms and molecules joined to each other through blind chance. The world is the conscious act of a concerned God. This religious truth has its practical application as it provides the basis for an optimistic attitude toward the universe.

Consider the Adam and Eve narrative. That Adam was

created of the earth teaches man humility and prepares him to accept death. The fashioning of Eve from Adam's rib tells of the bond between man and woman. What more forceful or dramatic way to say that all men are brothers? All of humanity have common parents, hence all men are brothers.

Rabbi Akiba stated that "the Bible spoke in the language of men." Religious truth is stated in "the language of men," be it myth, legend, or parable. The religious teaching is then reduced from abstract preachment to an incident or experience which has dramatic impact and which can often be vicariously experienced. There is no better way of teaching, no sounder way of learning. What is Torah but "that which is taught," and what is the Bible but a book of instruction for righteous living!

The Bible, thus conceived and read, makes for creative study. The author makes a partner of the reader. He invites him to an adventure of exploration and discovery. The incident is experienced by the reader. He becomes part of it. It affects his life. A Jew, studying the Revelation at Sinai, stands at Sinai hearing the call of God and answering "I will obey, and hearken!" We become one with those who danced about the calf of gold, and learn about our weakness for the gods we create—and we are admonished to be on guard. The re-reading of a Biblical narrative is new adventure, holding forth new "promised lands" to be explored and conquered. We study the Bible, not to learn about others, but to know ourselves. To know ourselves is a never-ending, ever-changing quest and adventure.

The words of Ecclesiasticus:

> There is none that hath ever made an end to learning it, and there is none that will ever find out all its mysteries. For its wisdom is richer than any sea, and its word deeper than any abyss.

AND BOOKS THAT FOLLOWED

Second only to the Bible in Judaism's rich library of literature is the *Talmud*.

The *Talmud* is comprised of *Mishnah* and *Gemara*.

THE MISHNAH:

Side by side with the Written Law in the Bible, there developed the Oral Law which expanded upon the ordinances of the Pentateuch. The Oral Law was handed down from master to disciple, discussed in academies of learning, and applied in courts of law. The great national and spiritual crisis which followed the unsuccessful rebellions against Rome motivated Judah the Prince to compile, systematize, and reduce to writing the Oral Law. This compendium of laws, legal opinions and decisions and comments upon them is the *Mishnah*. It is not a code of law, but rather a digest of opinions which invite further study and discussion.

THE GEMARA:

Study and discussion of the *Mishnah* was carried on in the centuries following in academies of learning and courts of law in Palestine and Babylonia. The summary digest of this scholarly activity is called the *Gemara*. It is not at all dry-as-dust legal argumentation. It rather reports on the exciting adventure of the application of law to life, the disputations which grew out of diverse opinions and differing traditions and conditions—interlaced here and there with a parable, a legend or just a good story.

CODES:

The Talmud is not a code of law, but the raw material out of which codes are fashioned. It was not till the middle ages that Jewish law was organized and codified. The greatest code was the *Mishneh Torah* of Maimonides. The latest and currently authoritative code is the *Shulhan Arukh* of Joseph Caro, compiled in the 16th century. These, like every great Jewish religious literary creation, abound in commentaries and super-commentaries, added through the ages and still being written today.

RESPONSA:

If a Jew needed religious guidance he turned to a book. If he felt unequal to the task he turned to a scholar. There were times when the complexity of the law in question was such that even the scholar practiced caution. He then sent a legal query to a recognized authority who replied with a *responsum*. The responsa of the great scholars of all ages became part and parcel of the Jewish legal system. The responsa literature is vast and continues to grow as new conditions create questions of law neither faced nor anticipated by previous generations.

Talmud, Codes, Responsa all deal with law. While this literature was growing there developed alongside works which nurtured the spirit and the faculties of heart.

THE MIDRASH:

There are a number of compilations of biblical interpretation and legends, called *midrashim,* dealing not with law but with concepts, beliefs, and those thoughts and ideas which flow from the imaginative faculties. Homiletics—preaching in interpretation of biblical verses and incidents—is in the spirit and mode of the *Midrash.*

MUSAR:

Judaism is rich in ethical treatises. Some are lengthy compendia dealing with all of life. Others are on specific subjects. Yet others are brief words of advice or admonition in letters from master to disciple, or an ethical will prepared by a father for his children.

POETRY AND PHILOSOPHY:

Poetry, the outpouring of the heart, and philosophy, the cultivation of the mind, have added many volumes to the library of Jewish literature. The philosophy and poetry were of a religious nature. The former erected intellectual fortifications about the faith, while the latter expressed the innermost moods and yearnings of a people struggling to live up to the demands of an exalted and demanding heritage.

THE SIDDUR:

The single volume which is best known to the Jew is the *Siddur,* his prayerbook. It has been his daily companion for many centuries. In it he finds the vocabulary for conversation with the Heavenly Father. Through it he lifts eyes and heart to his God. It is at once a book of poetry, history, and law. It celebrates God's goodness in nature and history. It reminds the Jew of his privileges and speaks to him of his responsibilities.

The *Siddur* has had many editions. It has been translated into every modern language. Prayerbooks to suit the needs or moods of a particular generation, group, or congregation have been fashioned. But whatever the edition or adaptation, it is the book best known and most beloved by our people. More than any other literary creation or compilation, it speaks for us and to us.

It is told that the martyr Rabbi Hanina ben Teradyon was placed on the pyre wrapped in a Scroll of Law. His students asked him:

"Our master, what do you see?"

He replied: "The parchment is being consumed by flame, but the letters are flying heavenward."

Many scrolls were put to the torch. Books were burned by those who sought to extinguish the light which came from Sinai. The Jew moistened the ashes with his tears. Having done so, he grasped the sacred letters and words to soar with them heavenward.

7

THE RELIGIOUS
ROUND

*Judaism is a way of life which en-
deavors to transform virtually every
human action into a means of communion with God.*

RABBI LOUIS FINKELSTEIN

IN ALL THY WAYS KNOW HIM

The rabbis taught:
  What brief statement contains within itself the main tenets of
the Torah?

In all thy ways know him

It means: Even in those things which you do for the needs
of your body, know God, and do these things for the sake of
His blessed Name. As for example, in food and drink, in
walking and in sitting, in lying down and in rising up, and in
conversation. All the needs of your body should be turned to
the worship of God, or to that which leads to His worship.

Just as God reveals Himself in every manifestation of nature,
so man is commanded to express his dependence and devotion
in every act of daily living.

God and man are in constant confrontation. "I have set the
Lord always before me," the Psalmist says for the believer. The
Jew establishes communion with his Creator, not only in word
but through deed—particularly through his deeds. God in
His goodness has indicated in the Torah how man may serve
Him. Generations of Jews in their adoration of the Divine have
added custom and ceremony, rite and ritual, so that they might
worship their God every day, the whole day, in every way.

The first words of the Jewish Code of Law, the *Shulhan
Arukh,* urge the Jew to "strengthen himself as a lion to rise
early in the morning to serve his Creator." And serve Him he
can, throughout the day and every day of his life. Judaism has
turned ordinary deeds of the common life into vehicles of
worship. The clothes he wears, the food he eats; the contents
of his conversation and the tone of his voice, his conduct at

home and in the market place—these and all else he does, from the "rising of the sun to the going down thereof," can all be turned into rites of relationship to God. Every act of man can be lifted to the service of God, if man dedicates the act to God. He can do so by asking: "What does God demand of me in these circumstances, in this matter, in this deed?" Judaism not only provides the answers, it does more. Through a system of law and ritual, it trains man in attitudes, sentiments, and discipline which provide him with a moral conditioned reflex. He is made ready to react morally and ethically in whatever situation he finds himself, by whatever he is confronted.

The rules of conduct by which man is to live and the rituals which train him for consecrated living are called *mitzvot*. The literal meaning is "that which has been commanded." Good as it is for man to worship God as his heart directs him, it is better still to worship Him as He desires it. As Hanina ben Hama taught:

> Greater is he who does when commanded than he who does without having been commanded.

The *mitzvot* tie the individual Jew to his people, past and present, in the fellowship of common observance. When an American Jew recites the blessing before eating bread in the same language and words as does a Jew in Melbourne or Paris that very day, as did Jews in 12th century Spain and 8th century Babylonia, he feels a strong sense of kinship with them. Ritual enables him to express communion with God and oneness with his people. Rabbi Abraham Kuk wrote:

> Because of our reverence and affection for the people of Israel, we lovingly observe the customs of Israel even if they are not wholly based on divine revelation.

The ritual of Judaism is a body of action symbols of commitment to God. Milton Steinberg wrote of:

> a system of rituals which interpenetrates my daily routines and invests them with poetry and intimations of the divine.

Israel Zangwill saw their chief value as disciplines and as bonds:

> Our ceremonialism is a training in self-conquest while it links the generations and unifies our atoms dispersed to the four corners of the earth as nothing else would.

To Maurice Samuel they make for the moral "conditioned reflex":

> The rituals and disciplines that surrounded my childhood sensitized my spirit, made it permanently susceptible to the messages behind them . . .

The modern philosopher Morris Raphael Cohen spoke of the value of symbolism:

> I have come to appreciate . . . the symbolism in which is celebrated the human need of trusting to a larger vision, according to which calamities come and go, but the continuity of life and faith in its better possibilities survive.

Is is best summed up by Israel Al-Nakawa in his ethical work *Menorat Hamaor:*

> Religious observances are the practical aspects of the Torah; they are conducive to the preserving and the heightening of the ethical tone of life. They help to sanctify Israel as a people as well as the life of the individual Jew.

There is literally no end to the multiplication of observances. In the endeavor to infuse every act of man with sanctity, injunctions sprouted and customs multiplied. They extended, for example, not only to the manner of dressing but to the act of getting dressed as well. The motivation was the fulfilment to an exquisite degree of the injunction to worship God always and in all ways. Judaism became an all-pervading religious civilization, where every aspect of life was a spiritual expression and experience. It was recognized, however, that, in ritual symbolism as in economic enterprise, there can be a point of diminishing return. Multiplication often decreases vitality and leads to weary conformance and no more. In the 10th century Saadia warned:

If you perform a precept with impatience, irritation, and weariness, you blot out its reward.

Eight centuries later, the Baal Shem Tov reminded:

The important thing is not how many separate injunctions are obeyed, but how and in what spirit we obey them.

Before the Jew there is always the challenge to give expression to his religious sentiments through *mitzvot,* and to give life to the *mitzvot* by awareness, intention, and spirit.

FROM THE RISING OF THE SUN

While a man lies in his bed he should be mindful in whose presence he is. As soon as he awakes, he must be mindful of the mercy of God, blessed be He, in that He has restored to him his soul of which he had given Him charge when it was weary, and which He restored to him refreshed and invigorated, so that he may worship Him with all his might, and minister to Him the whole day, for this is the object of every man . . . While still in bed, one must say: "I thank Thee, O living and eternal King, because Thou has graciously restored my soul to me; great is Thy faithfulness."

The first brief prayer is followed by many prayers and benedictions during the course of the day. Thrice daily a Jew is to pray: morning, afternoon, and night. Rabbi Meir said that a man should recite one hundred benedictions during the day. The great majority are said during his daily devotions. What of the rest?

The Jew must become aware that the world which God fashioned for him is filled with things extraordinary and wondrous. Throughout the day he is to thank God for His good world. In the process of expressing gratitude he becomes aware anew of those things for which he should give thanks; and in that process his heart feels the satisfaction and joy that all these are his to behold, to savor, to contemplate, and to enjoy.

But man is busy all day long, doing the thousand and one things which life and living demand. How and when does he find time for awareness, contemplation, gratitude, and enjoyment? To assure that he would, Judaism instituted a system of benedictions. Before and after partaking of food there are words of gratitude. And more. There are special and specific benedictions for such experiences as:

> smelling fragrant plants;
> witnessing lightning, falling stars, or lofty mountains;
> sight of the sea;
> seeing a rainbow:
> seeing trees blossoming.

Each has its own quality. Each gives special pleasure to man. Each therefore has earned its own benediction.

A medieval Jewish moralist wrote that the benedictions say to the Jew:

> Be not blind but open-eyed to the great wonders of nature, familiar everyday objects though they be.

Not the least of the wonders of God's world are extraordinary men. On seeing a sage, learned in Torah, we thank God for "having imparted His wisdom to those who revere Him." For a secular scholar we speak gratitude to the Creator "who hath given of His wisdom to mortals."

How well Israel Zangwill expressed his appreciation of the system of benedictions:

> We find a very jubilation of life—a spontaneous lyric appreciation of earth; a joy in the fruits of trees, the vine, and the field; enchantment in the fragrant odors of barks, plants, fruits and spices; exultation at the sight of stars, mountain, desert, sea, or rainbow. Beautiful trees and animals, spring blossoms equally with scholars and sages, all evoke their grace and appreciation . . . Everywhere the infiltration of earth by Heaven.

The Jew must train himself in the knowledge and in the skills necessary for observance of the ritual law. This task demands expenditure of time and energy in preparation and in performance. But is there any better way to spend one's time and any nobler enterprise in which to invest one's energy than "the infiltration of earth by Heaven"?

THE TABLE-ALTAR

The house of a Jew is his sanctuary, its table an altar. The food brought thereto must be specially prepared in accordance with law. Thus the act of eating is spiritualized so that it becomes a religious exercise before the Lord.

Food permitted is called *Kosher*.

Prohibited to the diet of the Jew and called *trefah* are:

> The flesh of animals which do not have cloven hoofs and
>   which do not chew the cud;
> All sea food, save fish which have fins and scales;
> All birds of prey;
> Creeping things and insects;
> The blood of animals.

The permitted animals must undergo ritual slaughter by a *shochet,* a religious functionary specially trained therefor. The jugular vein is cut by an exceedingly sharp knife, so the animal feels the least possible pain. (The slightest nick on the slaughter knife invalidates it.) The animal may not reveal any signs of disease. The blood is washed from the flesh and absorbed by a sprinkling of coarse salt. Finally there must be absolute separation of meat and dairy products, in the preparation of the food, in storing it, and during the eating. There must be separate dishes for meat and dairy, and after a meat meal some time must elapse before milk products may be eaten.*

* For a listing and rationale of the dietary laws, see: *The Dietary Laws,* by Samuel Dresner and Seymour Siegel, Burning Bush Press, N.Y. 1959.

Why this regimen in diet?

Those to whom these, like other laws, are divine need no further reason. A variety of explanations, however, for the origin and value of the dietary laws have been suggested. Among them are:

They were a reaction against idolatrous practices and serve to remind us of our opposition to all forms of idolatry, ancient and modern.

The method of slaughter—its limitation to a specially trained religious functionary, the care taken that the least possible pain be caused the animal—is an expression of the concern over pain caused a living creature, and thus serves the Jew as a reminder of the quality of mercy to all. Reverence, as it were, is shown the animal, a creature of God. Its fate is to provide food for man, but the taking of its life is entrusted to a scholarly and pious man, one who will not become brutalized in the process.

Rabbi Ezekiel Landau wrote:

> I cannot comprehend how a Jew could even dream of killing animals merely for the pleasure of hunting . . . When the act of killing is prompted by sport, it is downright cruelty.

Many point to hygienic reasons. Any suggestion of disease makes the animal *trefah*. The unsanitary habits of the forbidden swine and shellfish render them disease transmitters.

These laws also have their disciplinary value.

Maimonides states:

> The dietary laws train us to master our appetites; they accustom us to restrain the growth of desire and not to consider eating and drinking as the ends of man's existence.

Finally, as Rabbi Joseph H. Hertz declares:

> The supreme motive is holiness: not as an abstract idea, but as a regulating principle in the every day existence of men, women, and children. "Sanctify yourselves and be ye holy; for I am holy" (Leviticus 11:44) was spoken in connection with forbidden foods.

We add an appreciation of the dietary laws spoken by a Christian divine, David Tappan, in a lecture at Harvard University in 1803.

> As if Jehovah had said, "I have selected you from and exalted you far above the ignorant and idolatrous world. Let it be your care to walk worthy of this distinction. Let the quality of your food, as well as the rites of your worship, display your peculiar and holy character. Let even your manner of eating be so appropriate, so pure, so nicely adjusted by My law, as to convince yourselves and all the world that you are indeed separated from idolators, and devoted to Me alone."

FROM THE CRADLE . . .

The first commandment in the Bible is "be fruitful and multiply." Man is to marry and beget children. Marriage is not a concession to the flesh, but a sanctification of desire and the fulfilment of God's demand. The Jewish attitude to marriage is perhaps best summed up in the rabbinic saying that among the first questions asked of a man on the Day of Judgment is "Did you marry?" and "Have you founded a family?"

In the marriage ceremony, the Seven Benedictions are chanted. They praise God and thank Him for making the occasion possible. We thank Him for creating the world and man and woman; love and marriage which gives sanctity to love. The spirit of these benedictions is as though the world was called into being so that man and woman may sanctify their love in marriage and establish families to replenish God's good earth.

A newborn girl is named with appropriate ceremony in the synagogue. A boy enters the Covenant of Abraham through circumcision on the eighth day of his life. When he reaches his thirteenth birthday, he becomes a *bar mitzvah*. He has reached his religious majority. He may now be counted in the quorum of ten needed for public worship. He may be called to pronounce the benedictions at the Torah when it is read in the synagogue. At weekday service he will now don *tefillin* (phylacteries, squares of leather, which contain paragraphs from the Bible). At a special ceremony on the Sabbath, he is called to the Torah, recites the Torah blessings and chants a passage from the Prophets. This signifies to the congregation that he has reached his religious majority and that he has attained certain knowledge and familiarity with the liturgy. He is then festively welcomed as an adult member of the faith.

In many congregations, of late, a similar ceremony has been instituted for girls, called *bat mitzvah.*

Confirmation exercises are held two or three years later in Reform and Conservative congregations, when young men and women affirm their loyalty to their faith. These are held on or about the festival of *Shavuot,* which commemorates the giving of the Law at Sinai.

THE JEWISH HOME

Great emphasis has always been placed on the quality of Jewish family life. The home and the life of the family within it were considered the most effective school for training in Jewish attitudes, sentiments, and practices. The doors were always open wide for those who sought its shelter. To bring a stranger home for the Sabbath meal was a satisfying accomplishment. In centers of learning, families vied for the privilege of supplying board to needy students. The home was sanctified throughout the day by the prayers recited there and by the many blessings which accompanied almost every form of human activity. Ritual engaged in by all members of the family, and ceremonies celebrated by the family as a unit welded mother, father, son, and daughter into a consecrated band, joined to each other in sacred service and in joyous celebration.

Eliphaz prayed for Job, "And thou shalt know that thy tent is in peace." The Talmud comments:

> It refers to him who loves his wife as himself and honors her more than himself, who leads his children in the right path, and arranges for their early marriage.

Observers of the contemporary scene have been lavish in praise of the Jewish home and family. Thus Prof. H. A. Woodruff writes:

> One very strong element in Jewish cultures is the cohesiveness of the Hebrew family . . . Modern living conditions are sometimes blamed for the so-called break-up of the American home. It is significant, however, that the solidarity of the Jewish home has triumphed over the necessities of cliff-dwelling.

Having become a "cliff-dweller" in twentieth century western society, the Jew is made aware of the problems which inhere thereto . . . "Jewish communal leaders," writes Professor Salo W. Baron, "will . . . have to pay much more attention to the family. It will not do to go about rhapsodizing over the sweetness and purity of medieval family life." Every sizable Jewish community in America today has a Family Service Bureau and rabbis spend a good part of their time counseling on problems which beset the family.

The Jewish home is symbolized by the *mezuzah* on the doorposts. It contains an inscription on parchment of the section of the Bible beginning with "Hear, Oh, Israel, the Lord our God, the Lord is One." A decorative covering encases the parchment. The *mezuzah,* like a display sign on a business establishment, tells the nature of the enterprise within. It proclaims that here lives a family devoted to Torah. For the residents of the house, it serves as a constant reminder, "in their going out and in their coming in," that God's presence is everywhere, and that the home they have just left or are about to enter is what every home should be—a miniature sanctuary.

IN TIME OF SORROW

When the family unit is broken by death, the surviving members remain at home in mourning for seven days following the funeral. Friends and neighbors visit to express their sympathy and thus share the grief. On taking leave of mourners, we say, "May the Lord comfort you in the company of those who mourn for Zion and Jerusalem." The presence of friends and their words of consolation give strength to those in mourning, saying to them, as it were: "Every child of man is a mourner. Your loss is more immediate and your grief is therefore greatest. But whenever you are in the company of man, you are in the midst of mourners. See, they have risen out of their sorrow to live on normally and creatively. Strengthen yourself to do the same."

During the week of mourning, which is called *shivah,* services are conducted in the house of mourning. Often after the prescribed liturgy, a study session is conducted. This is the opportunity for Judaism to speak to the mourners offering them consolation and guidance.

The mourner recites a special prayer, the Kaddish, at every service of worship for eleven months, and on the anniversary of the death every year thereafter. *Kaddish* means sanctification. It does not deal with death but with life. Through its recitation the mourner expresses his acceptance of God's will, as he says:

> Magnified and sanctified be the great name of God throughout the world which He created according to His will.

It also proclaims the coming of God's kingdom on earth, thus speaking to the mourner of the great work ahead for every man and all mankind. He is bidden to rise above his sorrow, to eschew despair, and to take up his post in the company of men laboring to establish God's kingdom of peace.

RITUAL AND SERVICE

Important as ritual is to Judaism, it is regarded only as a means to an end. It is a symbol of piety rather than piety itself. An anecdote about the saintly Rabbi Israel Salanter places the matter in proper perspective.

Before partaking of a meal a Jew is to fulfil the ritual requirement of washing his hands. Rabbi Salanter, invited to dinner, sat at the table as water was being carried to the diners by the serving maid for that ritual. The other diners used the water freely in washing their hands, making quite a show of their observance of the *mitzvah*. When the maid brought the pitcher to the rabbi, he barely wet his fingers and no more. His friends were astonished at his apparent minimal fulfilment of the law. Rabbi Israel explained:

"When you washed your hands, you were concerned with the ritual requirements. When I washed my hands, I was concerned about the serving girl, poor child. She has to go to the well, draw the water and carry it to the house. Can I practice piety at the expense of her strength?"

Important as are prayer and ritual, they are not the only way of worshipping God. It has been said in truth that they are primarily preparation for true service.

It is told that Rabbi Levi Yitzhak was once visited by a teamster who asked him whether he should turn to another occupation, for his own interfered with his regular attendance at synagogue.

"Do you carry poor passengers free of charge?" asked the rabbi.

"Yes," replied the teamster.

"Then you serve the Lord in your occupation just as faithfully as I do when I am in the synagogue."

8

SABBATHS FOR REST; FESTIVALS FOR JOY; AND DAYS OF AWE

The river of life . . . flows from birth toward death. Day follows day with wearisome monotony. Only the holidays twine themselves together to form the circle of the year. Only through the holidays does life experience the eternity of the river that returns to its source. Then life becomes eternal.

FRANZ ROSENZWEIG

THE JEWELS IN THE CROWN

Thou hast given us in love, O Lord our God, Sabbaths for rest, festivals for gladness, holidays and sacred seasons for joy.

If Jewish life is a road, the holidays are wayside stops, for consideration of where the traveler has been and for refreshment and direction for the journey ahead. The Jew, assembled with his family around the festive board, begins the celebration of the day by lifting a goblet of wine and thanking God for the gift of "sacred seasons." He does so in the words of *Kiddush,* the hymn of sanctification. Wine is the symbol of joy; a family rising in gratitude to God bring holiness to the occasion. Sanctity and joy are the atmosphere and spirit of our holy days.

The holidays are the jewels in the crown of Judaism. They add beauty to the life of a people whose vocation is to proclaim the sovereignty of God. Each holiday presents an attribute of God. Some celebrate a historic event in the history of our people. All add a dimension of religious experience to the life of the individual Jew. They elevate man above the rest of creation, liberating him from the chains of nature which bind him to unceasing labor, and the chains of time which tie him to the here and now. He desists from labor, and soars through heart and mind to spheres of spiritual delight. He breaks the bonds of time as he relives experiences of ages past and envisions with the prophets the "end of days."

Through the holidays, the Jew celebrates the goodness of God, the life of his people, and his own free adventurous spirit and exalted destiny as child and as co-worker with God.

"Devote your festival half to yourself and half to God," was the advice of Rabbi Joshua ben Hanania. So the day is spent in prayer and study, but also in feasting and rejoicing. The joy of His children is a source of satisfaction to the Father. "Food, drink, and clean clothes bring honor to the holiday." But even in his moments of legitimate joy, the Jew cannot escape his responsibilities to fellow man. Maimonides urged caution:

> To eat and drink on a festival in the company of your family, without providing for the poor and the distressed, is not the "joy of the *mitzvah*" but the joy of your stomachs. It is a disgrace.

In the proper observance of the festivals, he recognized a great social good, for it promotes "the good feeling that men should have to each other in their social and political relations."

Philo, the philosopher of Alexandria, would call each day a holiday and all of life a celebration. But there are days which have been invested with heightened religious significance. Which are they and what do they celebrate?

THE SABBATH

A Talmudic legend tells of the Sabbath complaining before God, that all other days of the week had been given a mate save the Sabbath. "Very well," the Lord is said to have replied, "the Jewish people will be your mate." The Sabbath and the people Israel are bound together in love, united in wedlock, as it were, with God as the divine matchmaker.

To what purpose did God grant the gift of the Sabbath to His people?

In the Bible God gives the answer: "It is a sign between me and the children of Israel forever."

How does the Sabbath symbolize the relationship between God and man? Rest on the Sabbath and its dedication to spiritual pursuits is a sign that man has risen above his animal needs and toward God.

The Sabbath points to the cosmic partnership of man and God. That which God did ordain man is to retain. In Genesis we read: "God blessed the seventh day and hallowed it." In Exodus it is written: "Remember the Sabbath day to keep it holy." The Sabbath is holy because God made it holy. Man's task is to keep it holy. The Sabbath is holy because God made it so, yet man must sanctify it.

The Sabbath is ushered in with the *Kiddush,* the prayer of Sanctification.

> Blessed art thou, O Lord our God, King of the universe, who hast hallowed us by Thy commandments and hast taken pleasure in us, and in love and favor hast given us Thy holy Sabbath as an inheritance, a memorial of the creation. It is the first of the holy convocations, in remembrance of our departure from Egypt . . .

The Kiddush celebrates God as Creator of the world and of man. It reminds man that God Himself, as it were, rested on the seventh day, when His labors of creation were done. It thereby commands man to do the same. God delivered His people from the bondage of labor; man must free himself weekly from enslavement to his earthly pursuits. What God has done, man must continue to do. It is a sign between God and man forever.

In the ancient world, two peoples recognized the need for leisure. The answer of the Greek was a large slave class which gave the Athenian citizen all the time he needed for comfort and contemplation. The answer of the Jew was the Sabbath, a day on which every one would rest, for all, no matter what their station in life, were children of the same heavenly Father. The fourth of the Ten Commandments as re-stated in the Book of Deuteronomy reads:

> Six days shalt thou labor and do all thy work; but the seventh day is a sabbath unto the Lord Thy God; in it thou shalt not do any manner of work, thou, nor thy son, nor thy daughter, nor thy man-servant, nor thy maid-servant, nor thine ox, nor thine ass, nor any of thy cattle, nor thy stranger that is within thy gates; *that thy man-servant and thy maid-servant may rest as well as thou.*

It is to be a day of rest for those who most need rest, "thy man-servant and thy maid-servant." There is no more exalted vision of the rights of man, protected, as it were, by a merciful God.

"The object of the Sabbath requires no explanation," Maimonides wrote. "One seventh of the life of every man passes thus in comfort and rest from trouble and exertion."

The author of the mystic *Zohar* spoke of the Sabbath as "a mirror of the world to come."

In our day, Mordecai M. Kaplan sees the Sabbath as the day on which man, the creative artist of life, pauses in his brush work "to renew (his) vision of the object."

To Erich Fromm "the Sabbath is the day of peace between man and nature."

The need for rest is so important in Judaism, that God Himself is said to have rested when His week of work was done. It is further recognized that it must be a disciplined rest. The time and the manner of resting were prescribed by law, and the Jew ordered his life accordingly. It was decreed that it should be a day of joyful relaxation, of spiritual pursuits, and of mental refreshment. It was a day, as Philo said, "set apart for the building up of the spiritual element in man."

In all ages the Sabbath has kept the family together. Preparations for the Sabbath involved father, mother, and children alike. On the day itself, the family as a unit partook of the Sabbath meals and the day's ceremonies, sang songs, studied together, and engaged in the edifying and unifying activity of public worship. Because members of the family had to be together, they learned to live with one another. And what was true of the family on the Sabbath applied as well to the whole community who observed and worshipped in unity.

The Sabbath transformed the Jew.

Heinrich Heine writes of this transforming power in terms of a legend of a prince who was changed into a dog, but who from time to time resumed his princely state. So it was with the Jew. For six days of the week he may have led a harried existence, but on the Sabbath he became a prince, his home a court, his family royalty.

When was the ordered discipline and rest of the Sabbath needed more than today? Today, when the tempo of life frays our nerves, fatigues our bodies, and dulls our souls. And when everything about us conspires to tear apart the family unit, there are before us the rites and regulations of the Sabbath which for millennia have brought and kept the family together.

The Sabbath still retains its power of transformation.

The modern American novelist and playwright, Herman Wouk, found it so. In his stirring testament to his faith, *This Is My God,* he writes:

> Leaving the gloomy theater, the littered coffee cups, the jumbled, scarred-up scripts, the haggard actors, the shouting stagehands, the bedevilled director, the knuckle-gnawing producer, the clattering typewriter, and the dense tobacco smoke and backstage dust, I have come home. It has been a startling change, very like a brief return from the wars. My wife and my boys . . . are waiting for me, gay, dressed in holiday clothes . . . We have sat down to a splendid dinner, at a table graced with flowers and the old Sabbath symbols: the burning candles, the twisted loaves, the stuffed fish, and my grandfather's silver goblet brimming with wine. I have blessed my boys with the ancient blessing; we have sung the pleasantly syncopated Sabbath table hymns . . .
>
> We talk of Judaism, and there are the usual impossible boys' queries about God, which my wife and I field clumsily but as well as we can. For me, it is a retreat into restorative magic . . .
>
> The boys are at home in the synagogue, and they like it. They like even more the assured presence of their parents . . . it is their day.
>
> It is my day, too. The telephone is silent. I can think, read, study, walk, or do nothing. It is an oasis of quiet . . . My producer one Saturday night said to me, "I don't envy you your religion, but I envy you your Sabbath."

Even as we welcome the Sabbath Friday evening with the *Kiddush,* we take leave of the holiness of the day after sundown on Saturday in the ceremony of *Havdalah*. We chant blessings over a brimming cup of wine, a multi-flame candle, and fragrant spices, and praise God who makes distinction:

> between holy and profane; between light and darkness; between Israel and heathen nations, between the seventh day for rest and the six days for labor . . .

It is a reluctant leavetaking. How welcome and lovely was Sabbath rest! But note, the weekdays are ushered in by ceremony and blessing. They are not the holy Sabbath, but they too are the Creator's gift, and in them and through them we can sanctify ourselves by serving Him.

FESTIVALS FOR JOY

In ancient days, the faithful would appear at the Temple in Jerusalem thrice yearly, on the Pilgrim Festivals, *Pesach* (Passover), *Shavuot* (Pentecost), and *Sukkot* (Tabernacles). Their observance is in response to Biblical commandments. As on the Sabbath, one is to refrain from labor, but, in addition, each of the festivals has its unique character. Each marks a significant occasion in the yearly round of an agricultural society; each celebrates an event in the history of the Jewish people; each proclaims an attribute of God. Their celebration affords the Jew, today as in antiquity, an opportunity to fulfil the commandment "and thou shalt rejoice in thy festivals."

PESACH

Passover, the springtime festival, marks the miracle of nature's awakening to new life and growth after winter's death-like slumber. It celebrates the birth of new life too for the Children of Israel, who rose in this season to national freedom out of Egyptian bondage. The special liturgy of the holiday calls it "a memorial of the exodus from Egypt."

> Slaves were we to Pharaoh in Egypt. But the Lord our God brought us out of slavery with a mighty hand and an out-stretched arm. And if the Lord our God had not taken us out of the Land of Egypt, we and our children and our children's children would still be enslaved to the Pharaoh in Egypt.

Passover proclaims the Deity a God of Freedom, who championed His people's cause in their enslavement, even as He desires and demands for all His children in all times and in all places. Its message is a challenge to man to partnership with God in establishing and preserving a free humanity. The story of the exodus from Egypt has ever inspired the enslaved and persecuted, who heard its call for rebellion against tyranny.

An early proposed seal for the United States of America bore a picture of the children of Israel crossing the Red Sea and the inscription "Rebellion against tyrants is obedience to God."

Just as freedom demands eternal vigilance, so the ideal of freedom needs constant reaffirmation. Annually the Jew reminds himself and all who will listen what freedom is and what it demands. To instruct his children in Passover's meaning and message, a dramatic home celebration, the *seder*, is enacted. But even before the holiday, the child notes the approach of the season. The house is prepared for the welcome guest. All bread is removed, for in accordance with Biblical law only unleavened bread, called *matzah*, may be eaten during the eight days (seven in Israel and for Reform Jews) of the festival. On the first two evenings the family gathers for the *seder* service. It begins with an invitation: "All who are hungry, let them come and eat." (To give substance to form, contributions are made, prior to Passover, to funds which provide the needy with their holiday necessities.) Kiddush is chanted. A table-side service precedes the festive meal. Through song, story, and ceremony contained in a special book called the *Haggadah*, the meaning of freedom in the history of our people and in the life of mankind is taught to young and old alike. God is the central hero, urging, challenging, commanding man to rise above the deceitful "security" of slavery to the opportunity and responsibility of liberty.

We are asked not only to remember but actually to experience slavery and freedom. "Each man should regard himself," we read in the *seder* ritual, "as if *he himself* went out of Egypt from slavery to freedom." In a larger sense every celebrant of the Passover is bidden to identify himself with everyone who suffers in slavery. A Jew does not feel free himself if any one else is denied liberty.

SHAVUOT

Shavuot means literally a "week of weeks," occurring seven weeks after *Pesach*. It is a harvest festival which, in ancient days, marked the ingathering of the wheat harvest and the first fruits of the trees. The synagogue is decorated with greens and flowers as Jews join in the ancestral harvest celebration.

Of far greater significance is that this day is "the Season of the Giving of the Torah." It commemorates the Revelation at Sinai. God is proclaimed as Lawgiver. In the synagogue the Ten Commandments are read, those one hundred and twenty immortal words which have become the moral creed of western man. The festival celebrates the supremacy of the moral law.

According to tradition, *Shavuot* concludes what *Pesach* began. The exodus gave the opportunity for freedom, yet man might still be slave to his own desires and lower instincts. "Who is free?" ask the rabbis. "He who has committed himself to live by the Torah." Liberty without law is license. The acceptance of the Law at Sinai bestowed true freedom.

SUKKOT

The third of the agricultural festivals is *Sukkot,* the Feast of Tabernacles.

Thou shalt keep the feast of Tabernacles seven days after thou hast gathered in from thy threshing floor and from thy wine-press. And thou shalt rejoice in thy feast, thou and thy son, and thy daughter and thy man-servant and thy maid-servant, and the Levite, and the stranger and the fatherless, and the widow that are in thy gates. Seven days shalt thou keep a feast unto the Lord thy God in the place where thy Lord shall choose; because the Lord thy God shall bless thee in all the works of thy hands, and thou shalt be altogether joyful.

Sukkot thus is a thanksgiving festival, a time when the farmer in ancient Palestine would pause from his work, journey to Jerusalem, and in the Temple express his gratitude for God's goodness. The American Thanksgiving Day, also observed following the autumn harvest, took its inspiration from its Biblical counterpart.

The rabbis suggest that "altogether joyful" should mean "all together joyful." We do not fulfil the commandment until we are joyful all of us together—we, our servants, the stranger, the widow, and the orphan. In this spirit the Jew could not and would not celebrate a joyous festival until he had made provision that those less fortunate than he might also join in the celebration. God the Provider is proclaimed by the festival. An attribute ascribed to God is thus transformed into a challenge to man.

The ceremonial of this holiday is rich in color and meaning. The *etrog* (citron) and *lulav* (a palm branch to which twigs of myrtle and willow have been bound) are used in its observance. In the synagogue during the morning service of the festival a special blessing is said over *etrog* and *lulav*. A procession of men, each carrying these symbols of the "Season of our Rejoicing," proceeds around the synagogue to the chant of a special prayer asking that God's providential care continue to shelter and guide us.

Sukkot is the Hebrew word for "tents" or "tabernacles." During the holiday, meals are taken in small, frail huts, roofed with greens, erected for the occasion. This is in commemoration of the temporary dwellings of our ancestors in the wilderness on the way to the Promised Land, ". . . that your generations may know that I made the children of Israel to dwell in booths when I brought them out of the Land of Egypt." Again the Jew is reminded of the redemption from Egyptian slavery and man's dependence upon God.

A description of how the Sukkot festival was celebrated 2500 years ago in Palestine is found in the ninth chapter of the Book of Nehemiah. The people had just returned from the Babylonian exile. Ezra and Nehemiah taught them anew their faith, its ideals, its ceremonies, and ritual. The Bible records:

> And on the second day were gathered together the heads of the fathers' houses of all the people, the priests and the Levites and Ezra the Scribe; even to give attention to the words of the Law. And they found written in the Law how the Lord had commanded Moses and the Children of Israel should dwell in booths in the feast of the seventh month; and that they should publish and proclaim in all their cities and in Jerusalem, saying:
>
> "Go forth unto the mount, and fetch olive branches, and branches of wild olive, and myrtle branches, and palm branches, and branches of thick trees to make booths, as it is written." So the people went forth and brought them, and made themselves booths, everyone upon the roof of his house, and in their courts, and in the courts of the House of God . . . And all the congregation of them that were come out of captivity made booths and dwelt in booths.

The Festival of Sukkot is celebrated today in essentially the same manner as it has been for some twenty-five centuries.

The "Season of Rejoicing" concludes with *Simhat Torah,* the "Joy of the Law." On that day the last section of the Book of Deuteronomy is read, and immediately thereafter the first part of Genesis. Thus do Jews demonstrate that there is never an ending to the study of Torah, only continuation. The congregation celebrates the occasion in a joyful synagogue celebration with song and dance.

FEASTS AND FASTS

Two happy holidays were added in later days to our religious calendar. One, Purim, celebrates the deliverance of our people out of the hands of wicked Haman, as described in the Book of Esther. The other, Hanukkah, commemorates the successful struggle for religious freedom in the year 165 B.C.E., which is related in the books of the Apocrypha, *Maccabees I and II*.

HANUKKAH

During the eight days of Hanukkah a special prayer is added to the thrice daily services, which describes the background and meaning of the festival.

> We thank Thee, God, for the miraculous victories of liberation and deliverance which Thou didst effect for our ancestors in ancient days, during this season of the year. In the days of the Hasmonean, Mattathias ben Johanan, the high priest, and his sons, there arose against Thy people Israel a wicked Hellenic empire. It sought to make Israel abandon Thy Torah and to violate Thy precepts. But Thou, in Thine abundant mercies, didst come to their defense in a time of trouble. Thou didst champion their cause; Thou didst vindicate their rights; Thou didst avenge the wrongs they endured. Thou didst deliver the strong unto the hands of the weak; the many into the hands of the few; the corrupt into the hands of the upright; the wicked into the hands of the just; the arrogant into the hands of those who were faithful to Thy Torah . . .

> Thereupon Thy children entered Thy house. They removed the defilement from Thy Temple, and cleansed Thy shrine. They kindled festive lights in Thy Holy Courts, and they established these eight days of Hanukkah, in thankfulness and praise to Thy great name.

The eight days are celebrated primarily in the home, by kindling lights in a special Hanukkah candelabrum. One light is kindled on the first night and one additional candle added until eight burn on the final night. At the kindling of the lights, special blessings are said and hymns and songs are sung to celebrate this "Festival of Lights." Games are played, gifts are exchanged, and money is given the needy.

The story of Hanukkah is the tale of a rebellion against the Graeco-Syrian oppressor who sought to impose a heathen way of life on the Jewish people. For the first time in human history, a people fought for freedom of religion, for the right to worship their God. This first fight for freedom of conscience preserved for the world the knowledge of the One God. All who worship the One God owe a debt of gratitude to the brave men who raised the banner of rebellion against the Syrian rulers of Palestine over twenty-one centuries ago.

The message of Hanukkah is for all the world: to preserve, to protect, and to extend freedom of thought, expression, and worship; to resist to the death any attempt to diminish it.

PURIM

Jolly *Purim's* story is also added to the liturgy.

In the days of Mordecai and Esther, in Shushan the capital, when wicked Haman rose up against them, and sought to destroy, to slay and cause to perish all the Jews, both young and old, women and little children, on one day . . . and to take the spoil of them for a prey—then didst Thou in Thine abundant mercy bring his counsel to naught, didst frustrate his design, and return his recompense upon his own head; and they hanged him and his sons upon the gallows.

The *Book of Esther* is read in the synagogue. The mention of Haman is greeted with noise from *groggers,* for Haman represents all enemies "who rose up to destroy us." Wise Mordecai is hailed. Fair Esther, who risked her life to go before the king to plead for her people saying, "If I perish, I perish," is admired and praised. Merrymaking is the order of the day. The story is retold in drama, song, and parody. And the form of celebration ordained in the Book of Esther continues to the present day: "feasting and joy and the sending of gifts each man to his neighbor, and presents for the poor."

FAST DAYS

Four fast days commemorate the destruction of Jerusalem and the Holy Temple. Chief among them is the *Ninth of Av,* falling in mid-summer. According to tradition, the Temple of Solomon was destroyed on that day, as was the Second Temple in the year 70. It is a day of mourning. There is no eating or drinking. The Book of Lamentations, which tells of the destruction, is read in a mournful tone. Dirges add to the somberness and sadness. But a people which lives with a sense of destiny does not lose itself in despair. The closing elegies are love songs to Zion, and the mood is one of an unvoiced pledge to restore and rebuild God's sanctuary.

THE DAYS OF AWE

"Prepare to meet your God, O Israel" the prophet Amos urged. The Jew meets his God most solemnly and intimately on the holidays *Rosh Hashanah* (New Year) and *Yom Kippur* (Day of Atonement). In preparation for these sacred days, which tradition terms the Days of Awe and are today called the High Holy Days, the *shofar* is sounded at the conclusion of each weekday morning service in the preceding month. The *shofar* is a ram's horn fashioned into a musical instrument. Its piercing, plaintive sounds summon the worshipper to prepare himself spiritually for his rendezvous with his Maker. The period before the High Holy Days affords intellectual preparation for the emotional experience which these days promise. The heart is thus able to respond with mature and sober wisdom because it has been prepared by the mind. One senses, in the Jewish community, an atmosphere of increasing solemnity as the Days of Awe approach.

According to tradition, *Rosh Hashanah,* occurring in the early fall, is the birthday of the world. On this anniversary of creation, man stands before his Creator. He exposes himself to the Sovereign Judge in all his frailty, stating his shortcomings and asking forgiveness. As co-worker with God, man engages in self-judgment, in spiritual stocktaking. He is aware that there is no man who does not sin, and that sin can be erased by sincere repentance. Repentance begins with contrition but must continue as a recasting of one's life.

The two days of this solemn holiday are spent in synagogue worship. In the company of fellow worshippers the Jew finds strength to face his God and himself. The congregation unites in resolve to purify each heart and make God's presence manifest in His world through man's consecrated living. The service is marked by the sounding of the *shofar,* which rouses man out of his spiritual lethargy to rethink his days and examine his deeds. The congregation responds in the special liturgy of the holiday which proclaims God as Sovereign King, as the motive force in history, and as Redeemer of the world. The worshippers thereby obligate themselves in the year to come to declare God's Law supreme; to make God's will manifest in the lives of man and nations; to strive with all men of good will for the achievement of God's Kingdom on earth.

Rosh Hashanah is the gift of a new page in the Book of Life. Man may have sinned, but his own contrition which calls forth his Father's compassion gives him the chance to begin again. It is an auspicious beginning, commencing as it does with stock-taking, repentance and resolution.

We pray on this day:

> Our Father, our King, we have sinned before Thee.
> Our Father, our King, we have no king beside Thee.
> Our Father, our King, deal with us according to Thy will.
> Our Father, our King, renew unto us a good year . . .

There is no more awesome prayer than *Unetane Tokef,* recited both on *Rosh Hashanah* and on *Yom Kippur:*

We will celebrate the mighty holiness of this day . . .
Thy throne is established in mercy, and Thou sittest
on it in truth. Thou alone art Judge and Advocate
and Witness . . . Thou rememberest all things forgotten.
The Book of Records is open and the deeds therein
inscribed proclaim themselves; for lo, the seal of
every man's hand is set thereto . . .

On Rosh Hashanah the decree is signed and on Yom
Kippur it is sealed: how many shall pass away
and how many will be born; who shall live and who
shall die . . . who by sword, who by thirst, who by
hunger . . . who shall have rest and who will go wandering; who shall live in tranquility and who will
be harassed . . .

But man must not surrender to despair in the face of blind
fate, for this section is climaxed by the challenge:

But Repentance, Prayer, and Good Deeds can annul a harsh
decree.

Between the New Year and the Day of Atonement there is
a week of grace, a period for penance. During this time the
Jew prepares for the holiest day of the year. It is a day for
fasting and prayer. No food or drink is permitted from sundown to sundown, and the liturgy continues throughout the
day. It is man's appearance before God to plead forgiveness
for his sins. Tradition teaches that only the sins which man
has committed against God are forgiven by the merciful Father
on Atonement Day. For sins committed against fellow men,
one must seek and obtain forgiveness from those sinned
against, and make restitution if possible. In consequence of this
teaching there arose the custom that, during the week between
Rosh Hashanah and *Yom Kippur,* a Jew would call upon his
friends, neighbors, and associates, inquire of them if he had
wronged them during the year, and beg forgiveness. And if
one is asked to forgive, the law demands that he do so. When
a congregation joins for prayer on the Day of Atonement, it
is a company of friends who have made peace with each other

and have thus earned the right to approach their Father in Heaven for understanding and pardon.

Kol Nidre, chanted as the setting sun ushers in this most solemn of days, has become the most moving of Jewish worship experiences. Yet it is no more than a formula for the abrogation of vows. Why was this chosen to open the gates of heaven for prayer on this day? The answer is in history: It was spoken by individuals who through force had been made to take vows inimical to their faith, or who through frailty had vowed fealty to other gods, now come to the synagogue to retract and repent in the midst of a congregation of the faithful. It thus became an outcry of loyalty to the ancestral faith by the whole congregation—a defiant, triumphant affirmation of faith in the God of Israel.

Throughout the day the worshipper is reminded and taught what his affirmation imposes upon him. In the midst of his fast the words of Isaiah are read, which admonish him:

> Is this the fast I have chosen,
> A day for a man to afflict his soul?
> Is it to bow down his head as a bulrush
> And to spread sack cloth and ashes?
> Wilt thou call this a fast,
> An acceptable day to the Lord?
> Is not *this* the fast I have chosen?
> To loose the fetters of wickedness,
> To undo the bands of the yoke,
> And to let the oppressed go free,
> And that ye break every yoke?
> Is it not to deal thy bread to the hungry,
> And that thou bring the homeless to thy house?
> When thou seest the naked, that thou cover him,
> And that thou hide not thyself from thy fellow man?
> Then shall thy light break forth as the morning,
> And thy healing shall spring forth speedily;
> And thy righteousness shall go before thee,
> The glory of the Lord shall be thy protection.
> Then shalt thou call, and the Lord will answer;
> Thou shalt cry, and He will say, "Here I am."

As the day is drawing to an end, during the late afternoon service, the Book of Jonah is read. We hear again of the reluctant prophet told by God to go preach to Nineveh and save the city. Jonah, not wishing to spare the enemy, attempts to flee from duty, boarding a ship going to Tarshish. We learn with Jonah that God's concern is for all His children and His compassion extends to all His creatures.

> Then said the Lord: Thou hast pity on the gourd, for which thou hast not labored, neither did thou make it grow, which came up in a night and perished in a night. Should not I spare Nineveh, that great city, wherein are more than six score thousand persons . . . and also much cattle?

We hear of Jonah and ask ourselves: "Are we fleeing to Tarshish when duty should take us to Nineveh?" And as the concluding service, *Neilah,* closes the gates of heaven to prayer, we prepare to depart from God's House, cleansed and purified in soul, ennobled in resolve to fulfil our duties to God and man in the New Year ahead.

9

LAND, LANGUAGE, SYNAGOGUE

No matter where I go, it is always to Israel.

NAHMAN of Bratzlav

There is a vast storehouse filled with treasures. The key, the Hebrew language, is in our guardianship.

HENRIETTA SZOLD

The synagogue has been the most original and fruitful creation of the Jewish people.

ERNEST RÉNAN

Often in this presentation we have made reference to the land
of Israel, to the Hebrew language and to the synagogue. These
have been the "threefold cord" which have united the people
and have given vigor and vitality to the faith.

ZION, THE HOLY LAND

For a thousand years the Jewish people lived in Zion; for two
thousand years Zion lived in the people. The Jew turns toward
Jerusalem in his devotion and prays for its restoration thrice
daily. The *seder* ritual and the *Yom Kippur* liturgy both con-
clude with the hope and pledge, "Next year in Jerusalem."

The Holy Land has served as a magnet to the Jewish soul.
Abraham left home and homeland at God's behest to go to the
"land which I will show thee." It was the promise which sustained tribes of erstwhile slaves through forty years of wandering in the wilderness. In Babylonian exile the challenge of
King Cyrus, "Whoever is among you of all His people, may
the Lord his God be with him, and let him go up," was answered by fifty thousand who returned to rebuild the land.
Rabbinic literature is rich in laws, parables, and statements of
the people's love for the land. One senses a mystic bond between the People Israel and the Land of Israel.

In all lands of the dispersion the Jew longed for Zion and
made it a part of his life. His holidays celebrated harvest time
in the ancestral homeland. A visitor from Palestine was the
most welcome guest, joyfully greeted and lavishly honored.
With what eagerness did a community gather to hear his words
and how they were repeated and embellished for months and
years afterward!

And always there were individual Jews, some humble, many renowned, who returned. Others bemoaned their fate that they could not fulfil the religious law which ordained living in the Holy Land. At all times there were communities of Jews in Palestine. Their situation, often precarious, was at no time comfortable. Yet a steady stream of pilgrims and settlers made their way thither. The great poet-philosopher Judah Halevi, who himself set out for the Holy Land, expressed their feeling:

> My heart is in the East;
> I languish in the West.

The resolve of all the people in all the centuries of their dispersal was voiced by Isaiah of the Exile:

> For Zion's sake I will not . . . rest,
> Until her triumph go forth as brightness
> And her salvation as a torch that burns.

The longing for Zion was given political expression in our day. Its practical fulfilment took place in our generation with establishment of the State of Israel. But it was always more than the desire for a "publicly recognized and legally secured home in Palestine" for the Jewish people. It was also, or primarily, the conviction that in this land of prophet and sage the Jewish people would find, in the words of Ahad Ha-am, "a home of healing for its spirit."

Franz Kafka saw the return to Palestine of young *halutzim* (pioneers) in his generation as "a return to self, to one's own roots, to growth." The great chief rabbi of Palestine saw in the rebirth of the spirit the fulfilment of Israel's prophetic destiny. Said Rabbi Kuk:

> Only in the Holy Land can the spirit of our people develop and become a light for the world.

Even Theodor Herzl, the father of political Zionism, saw purpose beyond mere national interest:

> The world will be freer by our liberty, richer by our wealth, greater by our greatness.

Martin Buber, who through his writings has taught man how to meet God, and who through the personal example of emigration to Palestine has demonstrated to the Jew how to respond to his destiny, sums it up well:

Zion is memory, admonition, promise.

HEBREW, THE HOLY TONGUE

There are those who call the establishment of the State of Israel, by a people two thousand years exiled, a miracle. No less miraculous was the revival of the Hebrew language as a living tongue. Hebrew is as old as the Jewish people. It is the language of the Bible. In Biblical days it was spoken by the people as their common tongue. For the more than two thousand years since, it has served as the language of study and prayer. It was revived as the language of the modern Jewish national renaissance. Then, by a heroic effort of will on the part of one Eliezer ben Yehudah, it became the everyday language of the pioneers coming to rebuild Palestine. Today it is the official and the spoken language in the State of Israel.

Just as there was a bond between a people and its ancestral land, so there are unbreakable ties between this people and its old-new language.

It is venerated as the Holy Tongue. Dr. Louis Ginzberg tells of its sanctity:

The recollection that it was the Hebrew language in which the Revelation was given, in which the Prophets expressed their high ideals, in which the generations of our fathers breathed forth their suffering and joys, makes this language a holy one for us.

As constant companion of a people who lived with God, and as the vehicle through which this people addressed their "love letters" to Him, it became sacred to them. According to tradition it derives its sanctity from God Himself. Said Rabbi Simeon ben Pazzi:

> As the Torah was given in the Holy Tongue, so was the world created in the Holy Tongue.

It was the instrument with which God fashioned His gifts of compassion for His children—a world to live in and a Law by which to live.

According to Jewish law, prayers may be recited in any language. Yet Hebrew has persisted as the language of prayer. As Franz Rosenzweig wrote, "Jewish prayer means praying in Hebrew." In the flush of enthusiasm for synagogue reform in the mid-nineteenth century, Hebrew was all too often replaced by the vernacular as the language of prayer. In Germany this trend was opposed by Zechariah Frankel who argued:

> Hebrew is the historical chain which links all the dispersed parts of our people into one national body.

In this country, the organizer of Reform, Isaac Mayer Wise, pleaded for its retention in the synagogue.

> The Hebrew language in our public worship is the medium of our synagogal union. Dispersed as the house of Israel is in all lands, we must have a vehicle to understand each other in the house of God so that no brother be a stranger therein; and this vehicle is the Hebrew . . . In the house of the Lord let us always remain a unit, as our sires have been.

Frankel and Wise stressed the value of Hebrew as the unifying force for people and faith. Later, a founder of Conservative Judaism in America, Sabato Morais, gave added emphasis to their argument:

> The knowledge of Hebrew is the golden hinge upon which our national and religious existence turns.

It is the language of the loftiest creations of the Jewish spirit. It was born with this people and its faith, shared its vicissitudes, and is today part of the new life and vigor of reborn Israel.

Other languages have served Jew and Judaism well in their national and cultural needs.

Aramaic, *lingua franca* of the ancient Near-East, is the language of the *Gemara* and *Midrashim*. The leading Jewish philosophical works of the Middle Ages—Saadia's *Beliefs and Opinions,* Maimonides' *Guide For the Perplexed,* and the *Cuzari* of Judah Halevi—were written in Arabic. The Jews of the Mediterranean world spoke a Spanish-based language, Ladino. There is a modest literature in this language and there are those who speak it to the present day.

By far the most important and widespread secondary language of the Jewish people was and is Yiddish. Its base is Middle High German, with a generous sprinkling of Hebrew words and phrases. It has been the folk language of the Jews of eastern and central Europe since the Middle Ages. It boasts a rich and varied literature represented in every literary form from folk tale to novels of very high quality, from folk songs to prayers. In study, the text was in Hebrew or Aramaic, but the language of instruction was Yiddish. Prayers were in Hebrew but the religious discourse or sermon was in Yiddish. It became not only a valued cultural asset of our people, but also a useful handmaid of Hebrew for our faith. Said Rabbi Nahman of Bratzlav:

> When a Jew pours out his heart before God in plain Yiddish, that is a perfectly holy tongue.

The number to whom Yiddish is the mother tongue is decreasing. The vernacular of the country of residence is the everyday language of all Jewish communities. Hebrew remains, as it always was, the language of cultural and spiritual creativity and expression, and has become as well the living tongue of a growing and creative community in Israel.

THE SYNAGOGUE

Long before the Children of Israel reached the Promised Land, they built a house of worship. The Bible contains a full account of the building and furnishing of the Tabernacle which accompanied the people in the wanderings to the Land of Canaan. After the land had been subdued and settled, surrounding enemies defeated and the kingdom established, King David desired to build a Temple in Jerusalem, but was denied the privilege because he was a man of war. It was granted to King Solomon to raise an edifice to the glory of God.

At the dedication of the Temple, Solomon prayed:

> O Lord, the God of Israel,
> There is no God like Thee
> In Heaven above, or on earth beneath;
> Who keepest covenant and mercy with Thy servants,
> That walk before Thee with all their heart . . .
> Will God in very truth dwell on earth?
> Behold, heaven and the heaven of heavens
>   cannot contain Thee;
> How much less this house that I have builded!
> Yet have Thou respect unto the prayer of Thy
>   servant . . .
> And of Thy people Israel when they shall pray
>   toward this place;
> Yea, hear Thou in heaven Thy dwelling place;
> And when Thou hearest, forgive.

Sacrifices were offered daily, but Solomon spoke of prayer. For indeed the Jewish people learned to pray in its infancy and developed a capacity, even a genius, for prayer, as it matured. When the Temple was destroyed, the people was prepared to establish prayer as the form of worship. It was ready for the house of prayer, the synagogue.

How did the synagogue begin?

No record exists of the first house devoted to prayer and

study. It is generally assumed that during the Babylonian exile groups of those who "remembered Jerusalem" gathered together for comfort and strength. They reminisced about former glories and no doubt spoke of Jerusalem's Temple, now in ruins. Some Levites among them must have recited Temple prayers and chanted Temple melodies. There were no doubt learned men who read before the congregation from scrolls containing laws, records, poems, and prophecies. Gradually the meetings become regularized and their form standardized. Study and prayer became the agenda.

When the Temple was rebuilt in Jerusalem it became once again *the* House of Worship, but the rudimentary synagogues remained as well, for they answered the need of the people for organized prayer and religious instruction.

Dr. Louis Finkelstein attests:

> If Jewish life survived the destruction of the Temple that was because the Synagogue had been prepared to take over the whole burden and carry it onward for generations to come.

The synagogue was and is a democratic institution. No priestly class rules it. It needs no ministry to conduct its worship. The presence of a Scroll of the Law makes a room into a synagogue. Ten adult males form a congregation. Anyone able to do so may and does lead in prayer.

To the enigma of Israel's survival for two millennia without a homeland, some students of Jewish history suggest that the synagogue has been the "portable homeland" of the Jewish people. It has accompanied them to every place of their habitation, and has given Jewish communities and individual Jews the memories of the past, the strength in the present, and the faith in the future which provide morale for living. Leopold Zunz, in his great study on Jewish worship, states:

> The synagogue service was a rallying point to the Jews and proved the safeguard of Israel's faith.

Three Hebrew names have evolved for the synagogue. They are descriptive of its functions.

Beth Haknesset: Literal translation: a House of Assembly. To celebrate occasions of communal joy, to counsel together in times of stress, the Jews would gather in their synagogues. There, the individual would go in time of trouble to gain strength from being with fellow Jews, and in time of joy to heighten it by sharing it with friends and neighbors. The synagogue was a true community center.

Beth Hatefillah, House of Prayer. Judaism stresses public worship. Services are conducted in the synagogue thrice daily, every day of the year. On Sabbaths, festivals, and most particularly the High Holy Days, it is the lodging place of the Jewish spirit. Here the worshipper comes to commune with his God, to identify himself with his people, past and present, and to gain instruction and inspiration for life and the pursuit of holiness.

Beth Hamidrash, House of Study. The highest form of worship is study. In the service of worship there is provision for learning, and portions of the liturgy are not so much prayers as texts. In European Jewish communities formal adult study was conducted before and after services. Almost all men were members of one or more groups which met daily or weekly to study Bible, Talmud, or ethical treatises. The synagogue was a center of adult education, unmatched in width of participation and depth of learning by any educational institution anywhere. Of the three, the people in its folk wisdom chose *Beth Midrash* as its popular name for the synagogue, for in its eyes it was primarily and supremely a place for the study of Torah. Thus they echoed, in their own way, the description of Philo:

> What are our places of prayer . . . but schools of prudence, courage, temperance and justice, of piety, holiness, and virtue?

A word must be said about the nature of the American synagogue. Its program is to fulfil the traditional purpose of the synagogue, to be a community center, a house of prayer, and a school of learning. Today it is the meeting place of a variety of Jewish organizations; it conducts services, and places its greatest emphasis on its religious school for children. The present trend is towards more intensive education, with three sessions a week becoming the norm. There is now emphasis on education for the teen-ager and the adult, in formal classes or informal groups.

The chief functionary of the synagogue is the rabbi. He has no priestly powers or ecclesiastical prerogatives. He is a learned layman, who has by study and training been prepared to give spiritual leadership and religious instruction to his congregation. He is first and foremost a teacher as his title states, but in the complexity of congregational life he is called upon to fulfil a wide (and sometime bewildering) variety of functions. Judge Simon Rifkind, a perceptive observer of the Jewish scene, pointed out that, whereas in European countries the rabbi was a product of the community, in America the Jewish community is often the product of the rabbis who serve it.

The cantor (Hebrew: *hazzan*) is the trained specialist in liturgy and synagogal music who chants the service and leads the congregation in worship. On the staff of many congregations there are also a reader, to read the Pentateuch at services, an educational director for the congregational school, a youth leader for cultural and social activities, and an executive secretary charged with administrative responsibilities.

Judaism is a religious civilization, encompassing a wide spectrum of religious, cultural, and fellowship interests and activities. The program of the synagogue is fashioned to meet the varied needs of American Israel.

A congregation is an independent body. Authority is legally vested in its Board of Trustees. In practice, the widest influence is wielded by the rabbi and professional staff in the areas of their competence. Almost all congregations are affiliated with one of three synagogal associations, which reflect the threefold division in Jewish religious life in America. They are not separate religious denominations but rather approaches to Judaism, diverse in their ideology and practice. There is, however, considerable mobility from one group to the other.

How would one know whether he is in an Orthodox, Conservative or Reform synagogue?

ORTHODOX:

Services on Sabbaths, holidays, and daily. Main service on Saturday morning. Separation of sexes is usual at services either by balcony or partition. Men have head covering (as a sign of respect in the presence of God) and at morning services wear a *tallit* (prayer-shawl, the "fringed garment" of Biblical origin). The prayers are all in Hebrew. The cantor faces the ark, his back to the congregation. If there is a choir, it is of male voices only. No instrumental music accompanies the service.

Such a synagogue will generally affiliate with the Union of Orthodox Jewish Congregations and its rabbi is a member of the Rabbinical Council of America.

REFORM:

Services on the Sabbath and holidays. The main service is generally on Friday evening. Men and women sit together. Men do not have heads covered nor do they wear a *tallit*. Instrumental music accompanies a mixed choir. The *Hebrew Union Prayer Book* is used and the prayers are largely in English.

The Reform synagogue, usually called temple, is affiliated with the Union of American Hebrew Congregations; its rabbi is a member of the Central Conference of American Rabbis and was ordained by the Hebrew Union College—Jewish Institute of Religion.

CONSERVATIVE:

Services on Sabbath, holidays and daily. Main service either Saturday morning or Friday evening. Mixed seating at services. Men wear head covering and *tallit*. The cantor generally faces the congregation. The prayers are largely in Hebrew with a generous sprinkling of English readings. The choir may be of male and female voices. The majority of congregations do not use instrumental music at services. The rabbi, ordained at the Jewish Theological Seminary of America, is a member of the Rabbinical Assembly of America. The congregation is affiliated with the United Synagogue.

The synagogal bodies unite for consultation and joint action in The Synagogue Council of America.

The American Jew, feeling himself part of a religious community, has made the synagogue his expression of Jewish association. It gives him roots in his past, status in the present, and a sense of destiny for the future.

A Christian scholar of Judaism, R. Travers Herford, wrote:

> In all their long history the Jewish people have done scarcely anything more wonderful than to create the synagogue. No human institution has a longer continuous history and none has done more for the uplifting of the human race.

10

THE CHOSEN PEOPLE, OTHER FAITHS, AND THE WORLD TO COME

The Greek grasped the present moment, and was the artist; the Jew worshipped the timeless spirit and was the prophet.

ISAAC MAYER WISE

The election of Israel has never meant the rejection of mankind.

ROBERT GORDIS

I believe with perfect faith in the coming of the Messiah.

MAIMONIDES

THOU HAST CHOSEN US

When the Torah is read in the synagogue, a number of men come to the pulpit at stated intervals to pronounce the Benediction:

> Blessed art Thou, O Lord our God, King of the
> universe, who hast chosen us from all peoples,
> and hast given us Thy Torah. Blessed are Thou,
> O Lord, giver of the Torah.

When the Jew affirms that he is a member of a chosen people, what is he in effect saying?

No concept has been more misunderstood by friends, and none more mischievously used by enemies.

This benediction, like other statements of chosenness, is not said as a boast against others but as a challenge to ourselves. A more faithful rendering of the spirit of the blessing would read:

> . . . who has chosen us from all peoples by giving us Thy
> Torah.

The obligations imposed by the demands of the Torah laws have made us a "chosen people." As Edmond Fleg has stated:

> In charging itself with the burden of His law, Israel feels
> itself chosen not as a master, but as a servant.

The same sentiment has been variously expressed in our tradition. Maimonides, in his *Letter to the Jews of Yemen,* reminded them that "God had made us a unique people through His laws and precepts." The Rabbi of Apt spoke it in a homily:

> When God bade Abraham leave his father's house, He
> promised to make him a "great nation." The Evil Urge ob-
> served with what eagerness he prepared himself for the
> journey and whispered to him:

"You are doing the right thing. A great nation—that means power, that means possessions!"

But Abraham laughed at him. "I understand better than you," he said. "A great nation means a people that sanctifies the name of God."

To the people of the Kingdom of Israel, inclined in his day toward chauvinism, the prophet Amos spoke God's words:

Are ye not as the children of the Ethiopians unto me, O children of Israel!

And he taught them what chosenness means:

You only have I known of all the families of the earth; therefore will I visit upon you all your iniquities.

Israel's chosenness is that of a beloved gifted child, of whom the Father demands most in effort and accomplishment. The understanding child accepts it, not as a privilege, but as a responsibility. Samson Raphael Hirsch explained:

The Bible terms Israel "God's own people," but that does not imply Israel's exclusive possession of divine love and favor. On the contrary, it means that God has exclusive claim to Israel's service.

The relationship of God and Israel is through a Covenant. "I will take you to be my people, and I will be to you a God." The Covenant relationship as it is spelled out is conditional. We are His people, so long as we proclaim Him through our lives to be our God. He has chosen and we have also chosen. Rabbi Johanan ben Nappaha taught:

The Holy One offered the Torah to all nations, and none but Israel accepted it.

It was the conscious choice of accepting for itself the demands and discipline of the Torah that made Israel a chosen people. Its response to God's call conferred upon Israel its distinction. Since Israel is in constant confrontation with God, it must continue to reaffirm its choice at Sinai. "A chosen people," said Zangwill, "is really a choosing people." It is of God that Israel is a chosen people, yet it must through its will and life make itself God's "peculiar treasure" among the nations. Here again the paradox of man's relationship to God: that which is of God, must yet become so through man.

"How odd of God to choose the Jews," mused a cynic.
To which the reply: "It's not so odd. The Jews chose God."

The chosenness of Israel is also understood as a choice of vocation. God's concern is with spirituality, morality, and ethics. Israel declared itself to be His chosen people when it made these concerns the center of its being and destiny. Its ambition was to become a "kingdom of priests and a holy nation." How did it conceive its destiny? In the midst of Babylonian exile, when so many cried "our hope is lost . . . we are utterly cut off," Isaiah of the Exile reiterated and emphasized Israel's role in history:

I the Lord have called thee in righteousness and have taken hold of thine hand and kept thee, and set thee for a covenant of the people, for a light unto the nations; to open the blind eyes, to bring out the prisoners from the dungeon, and them that sit in darkness out of the prison house.

What a grand vision! Israel is to become involved in humanity, to become a "suffering servant" of God, to serve His children by bringing them closer to the Father. "The election of Israel," said Maimonides, "means that Israel is a people dedicated to the teaching of the Unity of God."

Would not a Father concerned for all His children offer commendation and express love for the child who is dedicating his life to the chief concerns of the Father, for the welfare of all His children?

He speaks tenderly, lovingly:

Israel, my son, my firstborn.
I have loved you with an everlasting love.

Judah Halevi, a poet even when he was writing philosophy, presents this analogy:

Israel is to the nations of the world what the heart is to the rest of the body. The heart suffers the most for it reacts to the ills of all parts of the body. But the heart has the power to throw off the impurities and to send life-giving forces to the body.

The challenge is ever before us:

Ye are my witnesses, saith the Lord.

Abraham Joshua Heschel responds for Israel:

We are God's stake in human history. We are the dawn and the dusk, the challenge and the test.

OTHER FAITHS

Why does not Judaism promote missionary activities? The answer was given by Moses Mendelssohn almost two hundred years ago:

Since . . . according to the rabbis, the just and virtuous of every nation shall enjoy eternal felicity hereafter, the reason for proselyting falls to the ground.

Mendelssohn was referring to the rabbinic dictum:

The righteous of the nations of the world have a share in the world to come.

One does not have to be a Jew to "enjoy eternal felicity." Salvation is not for the select. It is for all who have earned it. Who then are worthy of "a share in the world to come"? For gentiles the rabbis set standards which are called "Seven Commandments for the Sons of Noah." They enjoin the establishment of a system of civil justice; and forbid blasphemy; idolatry; incest or adultery; murder; stealing; inhumane acts, such as eating flesh torn or cut from a living animal. A gentile who abides by laws of justice and refrains from immorality, idolatry, bloodshed, and cruelty can gain salvation "outside the synagogue."

Judaism's view in this matter is best expressed in the well-known and oft-quoted statement:

> I call heaven and earth to witness that whether Jew or gentile, man or woman, man-servant or maid-servant, according to their deeds does the Divine Spirit rest upon them.

Judaism would not consider the other religions as equally true or good. Of its daughter religions it would object to Christianity's departure from pure and unqualified monotheism, and would look askance at Islam's fatalism and moral standards. But it would also consider them as partners in doing God's work.

Judah Halevi wrote that Christianity and Islam "are preparations and preface to the Messiah we expect." Isaac Lampronti in the 18th century said:

> Christians are not heathens. They believe in God and do not tolerate bloodshed . . . We must pray for their welfare.

In his chronicle of the expulsion of the Jews from Spain at the instigation of the Inquisition, ibn Verga wrote:

> I do not regard a Christian as a stranger, for he believes in divine creation and paradise.

A people who proclaimed God to be the Father of all naturally felt closely tied to other nations. For weal or for woe the world is one. The wellbeing of any people is a universal good. The suffering of any nation is a wound in the body of humanity. Judah Halevi wrote that the Jewish people felt this most keenly of all.

> Even as the heart may be affected by the disease of other organs, so Israel is affected by the troubles and wrongs of other nations.

In the Temple, on the Sukkot festival, seventy bullocks were sacrificed to atone for the sins of all the seventy nations of the world. The prayer of the hassidic saint, Rabbi Israel of Koznitz, is grand in its universality.

Lord of the world! I beg of you to redeem Israel. But if you do not want to do that, then I beg of you, redeem the gentiles.

In the end of things, in the fullness of time, national salvation will come through universal salvation.

Truth to tell, there was proselytizing activity in ancient times. We read of successful missionary activity in Talmudic days. The collection of ethical teachings, *Abot de Rabbi Nathan,* suggests that:

Every Jew should endeavor to bring men under the wings of the Shekhinah (Divine Presence) even as Abraham did.

A people to whom God's word was revealed and who through experience had discovered how to serve Him, felt it an obligation of love to his fellows who knew not the one God, to share the revelation and the discoveries. Those who chose to share this faith and way of life became Jews. A convert to Judaism is a full Jew in every sense of the word. It is forbidden to mention to him that he was ever anything else. Maimonides wrote to the proselyte Obadiah:

All who adopt Judaism and profess the unity of God's name are Abraham's disciples . . . Abraham is the father . . . also of his disciples and proselytes . . . There is absolutely no difference between you and us.

Many of the great of Israel were descended from proselytes. David the King, from whom were to descend all the kings of Judea (and according to tradition, the Messiah himself), was the great grandson of Ruth, born a Moabite.

Judaism recognizes that there are other roads which men and peoples travel in their spiritual quest. If the journey litters the road with maimed minds, scarred souls, or rack-broken bodies, it is an abomination and an affront before God. If the quest leads man upward in spirituality and onward in compassion, he is traveling a road which will bring him ever nearer to his Heavenly Father.

In her useful book, "Judaism and Christianity; The Differences," Dr. Trude Weiss-Rosmarin argues:

The notion that Judaism and Christianity, to maintain harmonious relations, must be "truly, basically one," is really a totalitarian aberration. For democracy is predicated on the conviction that dissimilarities and differences are no cause or justification for inequality. The democratic solution is that those of different views and beliefs should respect the dissimilar views and beliefs of their neighbors. After all, we don't demand that all Americans vote for the same ticket in order to promote national unity. On the contrary, we encourage political differences while expecting that those who differ will do so in a civilized and constructive manner.

What then are some of the differences in belief and emphasis?

GOD:

Judaism insists on a pure and uncompromising monotheism. God is One and His Name is One. Anything added compromises His Unity and subtracts from His Divinity. Schopenhauer, no friend of the Jews or their faith, wrote:

Judaism cannot be denied the glory of being the only genuinely monotheistic religion on earth . . .

God is spirit, not body. It is inconceivable to the Jew that God would assume human form. One of the *Thirteen Principles of Faith* of Maimonides is:

I believe with perfect faith that the Creator, blessed be His name, has no bodily form, and that no form can represent Him.

MIRACLES:

A Jew may or may not believe in miracles. Throughout Jewish tradition there has been the attempt to explain away or to minimize the seemingly miraculous. Suspensions of natural law described in the Bible are explained as natural phenomena or understood as allegory. Maimonides asserts:

The miraculous events associated with the careers of the prophets were part of their prophetic visions but did not happen in reality.

MAN:

Man is not born with taint of sin. He is endowed with potentialities for good or for evil. He need not be "saved," for he is not "damned." He can indeed lift himself toward God through his deeds. The Jew's purpose in life is not to seek salvation but to do *mitzvot*, good deeds. His life is the response not to the question "How may I be saved?" but "How may I serve?" He walks the world seeking out opportunities to serve God and fellow man which will give him fulfilment as a child of God by winning approval of the Heavenly Father. Both body and soul are from God. They are therefore holy. Man may not afflict either. They are in partnership in man and man is to utilize both for performing the will of God.

THE WORLD:

The world, this world, is the arena of life in which man is to fulfil his destiny. It is man's duty, imposed by God, to labor for the betterment of society, physical as well as spiritual. To withdraw from society is to escape responsibility. The road to God leads through active love for fellow man.

THE KINGDOM OF GOD

The Kingdom of God is of *this* world. The prophets spoke of the "end of days" as the ultimate stage in human history, when goodness and peace will reign supreme. Judaism is a this-world-centered religion. Man is here granted the opportunity to reclaim himself by participating in the ongoing, never-ending enterprise of redeeming humanity. We call again upon the authoritative spokesman for Judaism, Maimonides:

As for the Messianic era, it is in this world.

THE WORLD TO BE

The question is often asked, "Do Jews believe in life after death?" The answer must begin with a question, "What is meant by 'life after death'?" If we mean physical, bodily existence in a heaven or hell, the answer would be: There are Jews who believe so, but it is not an article of faith. If we mean immortality of the soul, the answer would be "Yes, this is a belief taught by our tradition."

There are no definite teachings in this matter. Beliefs and opinions vary. In the Bible there is only veiled mention of some sort of existence after death. But neither Pentateuch nor prophet make any reference to existence beyond this world. In Talmudic times the belief in life after death and in bodily resurrection was current. But there is a variety of statements on the subject in Talmudic and Midrashic literature expressing widely divergent views.

These differing views continue throughout Jewish tradition. Maimonides, the rationalist, writes:

> The hidden good in store for the righteous is life in the World to Come. It is life connected with no death, a kind of good connected with no evil . . .

> The World to Come harbors neither body nor aught of concrete form save only the souls of the righteous divested of a body as are the ministering angels . . . As the ancient sages say (in the Talmud): "In the World to Come there is no eating, no drinking, and no family life, save that the righteous are sitting with garlands upon their heads deriving joy from the radiance of God's Presence."

His critic, Rabbi Abraham ibn Daud, objects:

> "The World to Come harbors neither body nor aught of concrete form, etc." This man's words are in my eyes nigh to such who assert that there is no resurrection of body but of

souls alone. But, by the life of my head! this was not the opinion of our sages, may their memory be blessed, etc., etc.

And so the discussion continued and continues. An ancient sage said what was perhaps the wisest word on the whole matter. Quoting a verse in Isaiah, Rabbi Johanan ben Nappaha declared:

. . . as for the World to Come, "we have not heard, neither has the eye seen."

And also in the same statement:

The prophets prophesied only concerning the Messianic Age.

There is a popular picture in Jewish and world literature of the Jew waiting for the Messiah. Many Jews indeed, in every age, have had great faith in his imminent appearance. Rabbi Levi Yitzhak of Berditchev, in arranging a document setting forth the conditions and plans for a grandchild's marriage, wrote:

The wedding will be held, with God's help, a year hence, in Jerusalem, the holy city. But if, God forbid, the Messiah will not come during the year, then we shall have the ceremony, with God's help, in Berditchev.

Until modern times, the Messiah was eagerly awaited and many still await his coming. Conditions of life were often such that it was felt that only a wonder-working Messiah could save Israel and redeem the world.

Who and what is the Messiah? The Messiah we meet in the Bible is a member of the Davidic dynasty, a wise and utterly righteous ruler who will restore sovereignty to Israel, give it dominion and establish peace and well-being for his people. This concept of the Messiah is reflected in the Talmudic statement:

The only difference between the present and the Messianic age is our present subjection to the dominion of foreign powers.

But the vision of the prophets widened the concept to include the world and all humanity. Isaiah and Micah saw it as the age when all nations would acclaim the sovereignty of God's Law.

> When nation shall not lift up sword against nation, Neither shall they learn war anymore.

"When Messiah comes," said Maimonides, "war will end, God's blessings will be on all men." He elaborates:

> In Messiah's days there will be no hunger or war, no jealousy or strife; prosperity will be universal, and the world's occupation will be to know the Lord.

Indeed he warns:

> Do not imagine that King Messiah will perform signs and wonders . . . revive the dead, or do similar things. It is not so.

Clearly, we speak of an age in human history when men will have rid themselves of anger, hatred, strife; when true brotherhood will reign; when men will give witness through the quality of their lives, through the excellence of the society they establish, that they have indeed crowned God as King. This will be brought about in the Messianic Age.

When will the Messiah come? Who will bring him?

Maimonides has a strange statement:

> All the matters concerning Messiah's advent will not be known to anyone until they happen.

He says, does he not—look not for the miraculous signs. Pay no heed to those who claim proficiency in Messianic calculations. He would urge upon us the charge by the ancient sage, Rab:

> All the calculated ends have already passed and it now depends entirely on repentance and good deeds.

When will the Messiah come? Franz Kafka wrote:

> The Messiah will come only when he is no longer necessary; he will come only on the day after his arrival.

When men will have established God's kingdom on earth, then will it be known that the Messiah had indeed arrived. When men will no longer need to yearn for his coming to save them from tyranny, persecution, hunger, and strife, then they will know that he is here.

All men who labor to bring human history closer to its "end of days" when peace and love will reign, are they not each and all the Messiah?

Says Abraham Joshua Heschel:

An architect of hidden worlds, every pious Jew is, partly, the Messiah.

"The Jews," it has been said, "have a God who never dies and a Messiah who never comes."

The Messiah never comes, for he is already here in the hearts and lives of men. Men who stand before the living God and hear the charge and accept the challenge of the prophet to create a society where:

> The wolf shall dwell with the lamb,
> The leopard lie down with the kid,
> The calf and the young lion together,
> And a little child shall lead them . . .
> They shall not hurt nor destroy
> In all my holy mountain
> For the earth shall be full of the
>   knowledge of the Lord
> As the waters cover the sea.

THE TREE AND THE ROAD

A parable of Rabbi Nahman of Bratzlav

The Parable:

Each animal needs shade under which it can rest,
Each bird needs a branch upon which it can perch,
And there is strife among beast and bird for shade and perch.

There was once a group of people.
Said they to themselves:
If only there could be found a tree
In whose shade all animals could find repose,
Upon whose branches all birds could find rest—
They pondered and concluded:
    There is indeed such a tree!
And great was their desire to reach the tree
    For the pleasantness and joy there is boundless.

All animals and birds are there,
    Each in its shade,
    Each on its perch.
One does not hurt nor harm another,
    But they play together
    And romp with each other.
It is indeed happiness without measure to be there—
And the group began to consider how to reach the tree.

But argument broke out in the group,
    For there was none to guide them.
Some said:
    We must travel West!
While others:
    To the East!
One said in one direction,
    And another said in the opposite.
But they knew not the road nor the direction to the tree.

Came a wise man and said:
    Seek not the road or the direction, but ask:
    Who can reach the tree?
    For only those who are like the tree can reach it.
    The tree has three roots:
        Faith in God,
        Fear of Heaven,
        Humility.
        And the trunk of the tree is Truth.
    Only those who possess these qualities can reach the tree.
Such were the words of the wise man.

Not all in the group had these qualities.
Some did, many did not.
But there was great unity in the group,
    For there was love among them
    And they would not separate.
So they worked and waited until all had attained the qualities of
    the tree.

And when all had perfected themselves in
    Faith in God,
    Fear of Heaven,
    Humility, and
    Truth,
They began at once toward the tree.
As they were all now possessed of the same attributes,
    They agreed on the road and the direction—
    And lo—all roads and every direction led to the tree!
They traveled a way and saw the tree from afar.
    And they beheld: The tree stands not in one place.

For the tree has no place upon which to stand,
For place and space are of this world
    But the tree is above and beyond place and space
    For the tree is not of this world!
But if the tree is not in space
And not of this world—
How can the tree be reached?

Its Meaning:

The Tree: The tree is the tree of life, the life of peace and contentment which the prophets foresaw in Messiah's time in the "end of days," when

> None shall hurt nor destroy
> In all My holy mountain

All men yearn to reach that day and live that life: but men, being unprepared for it, dispute about the road, and argue about the direction—some saying East!
and others West!
But the road is neither to the East nor to the West,
Neither in this direction nor in that.

The road is in the lives and hearts of men. And should men attain the qualities of the age and that world—faith, reverence, humility, and truth—then the road would be found, for every road would lead to the world of end of days, where peace and happiness reign.

Yet, if such a world is not reached in your days, do not despair, neither sorrow nor mourn, for the glory of man and his salvation is not in the finding, but in the preparation for the journey and in walking on the way.

For the Jew—the Jewish Way of Life.

FOR FURTHER READING

Hillel the Sage challenged:
"Now, go forth and study!"
For further reading and study, we offer a select number of books, authoritative and readable.

GENERAL BOOKS ON JUDAISM:

Leo Baeck, *The Essence Of Judaism,* Schocken Books, Inc., New York 1948.

Leon Roth, *Judaism: A Portrait,* Viking Press, New York 1961.

Milton Steinberg, *Basic Judaism,* Harcourt, Brace & Co., New York 1947.

Robert Gordis, *Judaism For The Modern Age,* Farrar, Straus and Cudahy, New York 1955.

Robert Gordis, *A Faith For Moderns,* Bloch Publishing Co., New York 1960.

Louis Jacobs, *We Have Reason To Believe,* Valentine, Mitchell, London 1957.

David Aronson, *The Jewish Way Of Life,* The National Academy for Adult Jewish Studies of the United Synagogue of America, New York 1957.

David de Sola Pool, *Why I Am A Jew,* Bloch Publishing Co., New York 1957.

Philip Bernstein, *What The Jews Believe,* Farrar, Straus and Young, New York 1950.

Herman Wouk, *This Is My God,* Doubleday & Co., Garden City, N. Y. 1959.

For further reading on the subject matter of each chapter:

CHAPTER I:

Cecil Roth, *A Short History Of The Jewish People,* Jewish Publication Society of America, Philadelphia 1953.

Max L. Margolis and Alexander Marx, *A History Of The Jewish People,* Jewish Publication Society of America, Philadelphia 1927.

Solomon Grayzel, *A History Of The Jews,* Jewish Publication Society of America, Philadelphia 1947.

Howard M. Sachar, *The Course Of Modern Jewish History,* World Publishing Company, Cleveland 1958.

Rufus Learsi, *The Jews In America: A History,* World Publishing Company, Cleveland 1954.

CHAPTER II:

Kaufmann Kohler, *Jewish Theology,* The Riverdale Press, Cincinnati 1943.

Isidore Epstein, *The Faith of Judaism,* Soncino Press, London 1960.

CHAPTER III:

Samuel Belkin, *In His Image,* Abelard-Schuman, Ltd., London, New York, Toronto 1960.

CHAPTER IV:

From the Writings of Abraham J. Heschel, Between God and Man, Fritz A. Rothschild, ed., Harper & Bros., New York 1959.

The Writings of Martin Buber, selected, edited and introduced by Will Herberg, Meridian Books, New York 1956.

Mordecai Kaplan, *The Meaning Of God In Modern Jewish Religion,* The Jewish Reconstructionist Foundation, New York 1947.

Jacob B. Agus, *Banner Of Jerusalem . . . Thought Of Abraham Isaac Kuk,* Bloch Publishing Co., New York 1946 (Chaps. V and VI).

CHAPTER V:

Moritz Lazarus, *The Ethics Of Judaism,* Jewish Publication Society, Philadelphia 1900, 2 Vol.

Meyer Waxman, *Judaism And Ethics,* Thomas Yoseloff, New York, London 1953 (Section II—The Ethics of Judaism).

Israel Mattuck, *Jewish Ethics,* Hutchinson House, London 1958.

CHAPTER VI:

Bernard J. Bamberger, *The Bible: A Modern Jewish Approach,* B'nai Brith Hillel Foundations, New York 1955.

Louis Ginzberg, *Students, Scholars And Saints,* Jewish Publication Society, Philadelphia 1928.

Philip Birnbaum, *A Treasury Of Judaism,* Hebrew Publishing Co., New York 1957.

CHAPTER VII:

Louis Finkelstein, *The Beliefs And Practices Of Judaism,* The Devin-Adair Company, New York 1952.

Samuel Dresner and Seymour Siegel, *The Dietary Laws,* Burning Bush Press, New York 1959.

Hayyim Schauss, *The Lifetime Of A Jew,* Union of American Hebrew Congregations, New York 1950.

Ben M. Edidin, *Jewish Customs And Ceremonies,* Hebrew Publishing Company, New York 1941.

CHAPTER VIII:

Yaacov Vainstein, *The Cycle Of The Jewish Year,* The World Zionist Organization, Jerusalem 1953.

Ben M. Edidin, *Jewish Holidays And Festivals,* Hebrew Publishing Company, New York 1940.

Hayyim Schauss, *The Jewish Festivals,* Union of American Hebrew Congregations, Cincinnati 1938.

Abraham Joshua Heschel, *The Sabbath,* Farrar, Straus and Young, New York 1951.

CHAPTER IX:

Arthur Herzberg, *The Zionist Idea,* Doubleday & Co., Garden City, New York 1959.

Shalom Spiegel, *Hebrew Reborn,* The Macmillan Company, New York 1930.

Israel H. Levinthal, *Point Of View,* Abelard-Schuman, London and New York 1958.

CHAPTER X:

Trude Weiss Rosmarin, *Judaism And Christianity: The Differences,* The Jewish Book Club, New York 1943.

Abba Hillel Silver, *Where Judaism Differed,* The Macmillan Co., New York 1956.

Michael Higger, *The Jewish Utopia,* The Lord Baltimore Press, Baltimore 1932.

And for those who would travel further:

The Jews, Their History, Culture And Religion, Louis Finkelstein, ed., The Jewish Publication Society, Philadelphia, 2 Vol.

Salo Baron, *A Social And Religious History Of The Jews,* Columbia University Press, New York 1952-60, Vol. I-VIII and Index.

Meyer Waxman, *A History Of Jewish Literature,* Kingsport Press, Inc., Kingsport, Tenn., 4 Vol.

The Jewish People Past And Present, 4 Volumes, Jewish Encyclopedia Handbooks, New York 1948.

For References:

The Jewish Encyclopedia, Funk and Wagnall, New York 1901, 12 Volumes.

Universal Jewish Encyclopedia, Universal Jewish Encyclopedia Co., Inc., New York 1939, 10 Volumes.

The Standard Jewish Encyclopedia, Doubleday & Co., Garden City, New York 1959.

A word of regretful apology to the many able authors of valuable books on Judaism whose works were not included in this listing. Space may be infinite but pages, alas, are numbered.

Biographical Index

A

Abba Mari Yarhi (c. 1300), France, philosopher, 60

Ahad Ha-am (Asher Ginzberg) (1856-1927), Russia, essayist, 169

Akiba (c. 50-135), Palestine, rabbi, martyr, 26, 74, 99, 105, 132

Al Nakawa, Israel (d. 1391), Spain, moralist, martyr, 127, 139

Apt, Rabbi of, (Abraham Yehoshua Heschel) (d. 1822), Russia, Hassidic rabbi, 106, 180

Asher ben Yehiel (1250-1328), Germany, Spain, talmudist, 113

B

Baal Shem Tov, Israel (1700-1760), Podolia, founder of Hassidism, 42, 43, 107, 120, 130, 140

Baeck, Leo, (1873-1956), Germany, rabbi, 82, 97

Ben Yehudah, Eliezer (1858-1922), Vilna, Jerusalem, lexicographer, reviver of spoken Hebrew, 170

Ben Zoma (2nd century), Palestine, rabbi, 107

Brandeis, Louis D. (1856-1941), U.S.A. Supreme Court justice, 87

Buber, Martin (1878—), Germany, Israel, theologian, 13, 57, 66, 89, 170

C

Caro, Joseph (1488-1575), Palestine, rabbinic codifier, 39, 134

Cohen, Hermann (1842-1918), Germany, philosopher, 120

Cohen, Morris Raphael (1880-1947), U.S.A., philosopher, 123, 139

D

Dubnow, Simon (1860-1943), Russia, historian, 21, 22

I

Ibn Daud, Abraham (c. 1110-1180), Spain, philosopher, 188
Ibn Ezra, Abraham, (1092-1167), Spain, Bible scholar, poet, 35, 103
Ibn Pakuda, Bahya (11th century), Spain, moralist, 82
Ibn Verga, Solomon (15-16th century), Spain, Portugal, Italy, historian, physician, I, 184
Isaiah (8th century B.C.E.), prophet, 16, 17, 102, 190; of the Exile, 182
Israel of Koznitz, (d. 1814), Russia, Hassidic rabbi, 184, 185

J

Jeremiah (6th century B.C.E.), prophet, 17, 18, 102
Johanan bar Nappaha (195-279), Palestine, rabbi, 181, 189
Josephus, Flavius (37-105), Palestine, historian, 29
Joshua ben Levi (2nd century), Palestine, rabbi, 71
Jowett, Benjamin (1817-1893), England, classical scholar, 11
Judah Halevi (1085-1140), Spain, poet, philosopher, physician, 35, 68, 69, 96, 169, 172, 182, 184
Judah the Prince (Ha-Nasi) (135-220), Palestine, rabbi, editor of Mishnah, 28, 127

K

Kafka, Franz (1883-1924), Austria, novelist, 169, 190
Kaplan, Mordecai M. (1881—), U.S.A., rabbi, founder of Reconstructionism, 65, 153
Kolitz, Zvi, modern Israeli author, 81
Koretz, Rebbe of (Pinhas) (d. 1791), Poland, Hassidic rabbi, 94
Krochmal, Nahman (1785-1840), Galicia, historian, philosopher, 130
Kuk, Abraham Isaac (1864-1935), Russia, Palestine, Chief Rabbi, 65, 66, 93, 99, 138, 169

L

Landau, Ezekiel (1713-1793), Central Europe, rabbi, 143
Lazarus, Emma (1849-1887), U.S.A., poet, 38

Z

Subject Index